It Cost Me Everything

Kimberly Moses And Co-Authors

Copyright © 2019 by Kimberly Moses

All rights reserved. No part of this publication may be reproduced by any means, graphics, electronic, or mechanical, including photocopying, recording, taping, or by any information storage retrieval system without the written permission of the publisher except in the case of brief quotations embodied in critical articles and reviews.

Kimberly Moses/Rejoice Essential Publishing
PO BOX 512
Effingham, SC 29541

www.republishing.org

Unless otherwise indicated, scripture is taken from the King James Version.

Scripture quotations marked (NKJV) are taken from the New King James Version®. Copyright © 1982 by Thomas Nelson. Used by permission. All rights reserved.

Scriptures quotations marked (NIV) are taken from the Holy Bible, New International Version®, NIV®. Copyright © 1973, 1978, 1984, 2011 by Biblica, Inc.™ Used by permission of Zondervan. All rights reserved worldwide. www.zondervan.com The "NIV" and "New International Version" are trademarks registered in the United States Patent and Trademark Office by Biblica, Inc.™

Scripture quotations marked (AMP) are taken from the Amplified Bible, Copyright © 1954, 1958, 1962, 1964, 1965, 1987 by The Lockman Foundation. Used by permission

Scripture quotations marked (NLT) are taken from the Holy Bible, New Living Translation, copyright ©1996, 2004, 2015 by Tyndale House Foundation. Used by permission of Tyndale House Publishers, Inc., Carol Stream, Illinois 60188. All rights reserved.

Scripture quotations marked (ESV) are from the ESV® Bible (The Holy Bible, English Standard Version®), copyright © 2001 by Crossway Bibles, a publishing ministry of Good News Publishers. Used by permission. All rights reserved."

Scripture quotations marked (NASB) are taken from the New American Standard Bible® (NASB),Copyright © 1960, 1962, 1963, 1968, 1971, 1972, 1973, 1975, 1977, 1995 by The Lockman Foundation Used by permission. www.Lockman.org

Scripture quotations marked (ERV) are taken from the HOLY BIBLE: EASY-TO-READ VERSION © 2001 by World Bible Translation Center, Inc. and used by permission.

Scripture quotations marked (CEB) are quoted from the Common English Bible, copyright © 2010 by the Common English Bible http://www.commonenglishbible.com/. Used by permission. All rights reserved.

It Cost Me Everything/ Kimberly Moses And Co-Authors

ISBN-10: 1-946756-48-2
ISBN-13: 978-1-946756-48-0
Library of Congress Control Number:2019901774

DEDICATION

I dedicate this book to a lost and dying world that needs to hear the message of the good news of Jesus Christ. I would like to thank each co-author for believing in this project. I couldn't have completed this assignment without you guys. Together, we make a great team. Thank you everyone for supporting my book ministry. Many blessings to you.

Table of Contents

ACKNOWLEDGMENTS..xi
FOREWORD..xiii
INTRODUCTION..1

- CHAPTER ONE: ADDICTION
  by Kimberly Moses.......................3

- CHAPTER TWO: ADULTERY
  by Yolanda Samuels....................9

- CHAPTER THREE: ALCOHOLISM
  by Coretta Kelsey.......................21

- CHAPTER FOUR: ANGER
  by Angela Richardson...............27

- CHAPTER FIVE: DEPRESSION
  by Jennifer Jackson...................40

- CHAPTER SIX: DISOBEDIENCE
  by Joyce Hope............................50

- CHAPTER SEVEN: DIVORCE
  by Bridget Jefferson...................58

CHAPTER EIGHT:	DOMESTIC VIOLENCE
	by Joy Martin............................69
CHAPTER NINE:	ENVY
	by Kimberly Moses..................88
CHAPTER TEN:	FEAR
	by Anstrice Epps......................94
CHAPTER ELEVEN:	FORNICATION
	by Melissa Portis....................101
CHAPTER TWELVE:	GLUTTONY
	by Kimberly Moses................112
CHAPTER THIRTEEN:	GUILT
	by Kimberly Moses................118
CHAPTER FOURTEEN:	IDOLATRY
	by Carolyn Boler....................126
CHAPTER FIFTEEN:	INCEST
	by Kimberly Moses................135
CHAPTER SIXTEEN:	LUST
	by Kimberly Moses................140
CHAPTER SEVENTEEN:	LYING
	by Kimberly Moses..............148

CHAPTER EIGHTEEN:	MOLESTATION by DeWanda Ann Samuel.................154
CHAPTER NINETEEN:	PERVERSION by Zolisha Ware...........166
CHAPTER TWENTY:	PRIDE by Alex Harding...........176
CHAPTER TWENTY ONE:	PROSTITUTION by Kimberly Moses.......183
CHAPTER TWENTY TWO:	RAPE by Alexander Young.....189
CHAPTER TWENTY THREE:	REVENGE by Kimberly Moses.......195
CHAPTER TWENTY FOUR:	SLOTHFULNESS by Kimberly Moses.......203
CHAPTER TWENTY FIVE:	STEALING by Kimberly Moses......209
CHAPTER TWENTY SIX:	STRIFE by Kimberly Moses.......214

CHAPTER TWENTY SEVEN:	UNGODLY SOUL TIES by Maudia Washington	219
CHAPTER TWENTY EIGHT:	WITCHCRAFT by LaShana Lloyd	228

ABOUT THE AUTHORS..238

REFERENCES..268

ACKNOWLEDGMENTS

This book wouldn't be possible without the inspiration of the Holy Spirit. He gave me the blueprint and I just obeyed as I wrote the manuscript.

2 Timothy 3:16-17 says, "All scripture is given by inspiration of God, and is profitable for doctrine, for reproof, for correction, for instruction in righteousness: That the man of God may be perfect, thoroughly furnished unto all good works."

FOREWORD

First, let me say that I love testimonies because they show you how far the hand of God will reach to deliver His people. His arm is not shortened that it cannot save, nor His ear heavy that He cannot hear (Isa. 59:1). Testimonies give hope to the hopeless, set captives free, and break the bands of wickedness. They also reveal the love, mercy, and grace of God. Your testimony is for those who are sinking and need a life jacket. Some people are bound right now that need your testimony to break free from their chains.

This book is going to minister to people for years and years to come. As long as the earth remains this book is going to preach. No matter who you are or your background, you'll find yourself somewhere in this book. We've all fell short in one or more areas. I commend these men and women of God for sharing. When someone opens up and shares their ugly past, it's never about them. It's about God getting the glory and souls being saved.

While I was going through the pages, I was like, "Wow God!" I saw some things and I been through some things, but I was still amazed at what God brought these people out of. He delivered them out of all kinds of Strongholds. But they didn't just go through for themselves. They went through so that YOU the reader can be set free as well. They had no idea when they were in bondage, full of lusts, in perversion, in adultery, bound by addictions and other things, their life would become a message. I love how that message points to Jesus. So, there's no doubt about who set them free. Not only do they give you testimonies, but they give you scriptures as well. There are prayers also at the end of every chapter so you can read them and be set free.

As you read this book, you'll find something that you can identify with. Maybe you've been there, or perhaps you're there now. Either way, it will minister to you. If you're already out, it's an encouragement to stay out. If you're still in the thing, it's an encouragement to get out. No matter who is reading this book, God has you covered.

I can identify because I dealt with alcoholism, anger, depression, domestic violence, and fear. So have many of you. You might see yourself as someone the Lord can't use, or the Lord can't love because of what you've done, but God is RICH IN MERCY (Eph. 2:4). It's not by chance that you have this book in your possession. God is setting you free. TODAY, if you will hear His voice, harden not your heart (Heb. 3:15).

Tron Moses, Author of "Who Touched Me: My Journey to Jesus."

INTRODUCTION

Did you know that the wrong choices and sin can cost you everything? One mistake can wreck your life and ruin your legacy. A night of passion can destroy your family and more. Every day people are doing things that they later regret. They might react negatively and hurt someone they love. They might damage someone's property because they acted out in anger.

We all make choices in life. Are you making the right decisions? We choose what path we are to take. Are you on the right track? As we go on this journey called life, there will be ups and downs. How do you cope with pain? There will be good and bad days. How do you deal with conflict? We also choose if we want to have a relationship with Jesus or follow another deity. If you die today, will you make it to heaven?

We live in a sinful world. Everyday we can decide if we want to sin or live uprightly before God. We will look at various sins through this book and highlight the consequences. We will show you how sin can cost you everything! After reading this book, you will make better choices. You will also produce the fruits of the Holy Spirit. Your relationship with the Lord will increase.

Each co-author has a compelling story. As you read the pages, take heed unless you fall (1 Corinthians 10:12). After you finished reading this book, sow it into someone's life. Give it to your rebellious child so they can get delivered. Give it to someone who is deep in sin. Give it to someone who is lukewarm. The Holy Spirit will draw them to open the pages and read the content inside. There is a world out there that needs to know that, "Sin Cost Me Everything!"

CHAPTER ONE

Addiction

BY KIMBERLY MOSES

Have you ever repeatedly acted on something that you wished you could stop? Have you ever been so hooked on something that was bad for you? You can be hooked on gambling, sex, eating, shopping, stealing, drugs, alcohol, etc. which is called addiction. Many people have some severe addictions that are keeping them bound. The word addicted is having a compulsive physiological need for a habit-forming substance (such as a drug) or being strongly inclined or compelled to do, use, or indulge in something repeatedly.[1] In other words, you can't get enough of something, and you always seek opportunities to indulge again. Some people are addicted to sinful things, and they are on the path of destruction. Romans 6:1 says, "What shall we say then? Shall we continue in sin, that grace may abound?" Having the wrong addiction can cost you everything.

Now that we know what addiction is let's explore some of its consequences. There are various forms of addiction but let's keep it broad when we consider the following:

CONSEQUENCES

1. Loss of Money

No matter what kind of addiction you may have, it will cost you money. People that are hooked on drugs, alcohol, cigarettes, etc. will spend money to fund their addiction. For instance, a person who smokes a pack of cigarettes a day will spend around $2,000 annually[2] The average household spends about $565 a year on alcohol.[3] When someone has a drug addiction, they will spend their whole paycheck to buy drugs. They will start selling items out of their home or sell their body to get drugs. When someone has a gambling addiction, they will spend the bill money to satisfy their addiction.

2. Sickness

Certain addictions are detrimental to your health. You can smoke several packs of cigarettes a day for years, and it will catch up with you. When I was a Registered Respiratory Therapist, several of my patients had COPD. They couldn't breathe without bending over forward sucking air forcibly in their lungs. They had to walk around on an oxygen tank because their normal oxygen range was around 88%. They had a hard time exerting themselves without getting short of breath. They got short of breath when they walked up a flight of stairs or took a few steps on their normal routine. Sexual addictions can lead to STDs. Alcohol addiction can lead to liver failure.

3. Demonic Influence

When you are bound by an addiction that is causing you to sin repeatedly, then you are under demonic influence. You know something is wrong, but you continue to do it because you love the thrill of living on the edge. Once I heard someone say, "Sin is like a credit card. You have fun spending now, but you will pay later." 2 Corinthians 4:4 says, "In whom the god of this world hath blinded the minds of them which believe not, lest the light of the glorious gospel of Christ, who is the image of God, should shine unto them." It is not the will of God for you to be bound. Romans 6:12 says, "Let not sin therefore reign in your mortal body, that ye should obey it in the lusts thereof." Now that we have covered some of the consequences of addiction let's look at Tommy's story of how addiction cost him everything!

TOMMY'S TESTIMONY

Tommy and Nicole were married for several years. They had three lovely children. People on the outside thought they were happy, but that was far from the truth. Tommy and Nicole had a rocky relationship. They had been divorced two times and re-married. The main reason for their divorce always came back up which was Tommy's gambling addiction. Nicole worked as a hair stylist. Her work would fluctuate based on her client's needs. Tommy worked in construction. He would pick up new projects here and there.

Tommy would spend the bill money at the bar, playing the lottery, and on expensive cigars. When it was time to pay the bills, Nicole had to try her best to do everything. Many times, their lights got cut off. The landlord threatened to evict them because they were months behind on rent. The children were hungry because they were tired of eating beans and rice, ramen, hot dogs, and peanut butter and jelly sandwiches. Nicole was so angry at Tommy because this was a constant thing they had to go through. When she threatened to leave him, he would straighten up for a few days and apologize. However, he went back to his old ways.

Nicole felt betrayed, and she was carrying the burden of her family. She would work overtime and didn't sleep much to provide for her family. Sometimes, Tommy would leave the house for several days and wouldn't come back. Nicole didn't know where her husband was at because Tommy wasn't answering his phone. One day, Nicole decided enough was enough. She hired an attorney and filed for divorce for the 3rd time. Nicole didn't care. She was upset and hurt. Tommy begged Nicole to stay, but she refused.

Nicole and her three children moved to the next town over to get a new start. It was tough on the children because they had friends at their old school. They started to rebel but evenly straighten up when they saw how stressed their mom was. Months later, the divorce was finalized. Tommy was still trying to get his family back, but it was too late. His children hated him, and Nicole started dating someone else. Eventually, she remarried. Her new husband is an excellent provider and gives her a sense of security that she always desired. When Tommy found out about Nicole getting remarried, he was devastated. Gambling cost him everything.

GOD'S REDEMPTION

Tommy was broken and was lost. He tried to find happiness in the bar by drinking away his sorrows, but it wasn't working. He was tired of puking every day and having a hangover. He let himself go. He was no longer clean shaven, but he had a ragged beard. He was way overdue for a haircut. Every day, he would go through the routine of life. He had suicidal thoughts and was depressed. One of Tommy's sisters came by the house to check on him one day because she hadn't heard from him in a while. Her name was Linda. When she saw how awful he looked, her heart broke. She encouraged him. She made him something to eat which was the first home cooked meal that he had in months. Afterward, Linda told him to shower and get dressed.

His sister took him to the barber shop because he was starting to look like a cave man. Tommy sat down in the barber's chair. He had never had a haircut before from this barber. The barber's name was Shawn. Shawn was a Christian. He began having a conversation with Tommy and found out what he was going through. Shawn encouraged him and told him about Jesus. He invited Tommy to attend Bible study with him sometimes. When the hair cut was over, Tommy thanked Shawn. He looked like a brand-new man. Linda took her brother back home and said goodbye. Tommy couldn't get the conversation out of his mind that he had with Shawn. So, the next day he went to bible study. When he stepped into the building, he felt love and peace. He wanted to always feel like this. He realized how depressed he was and how he destroyed his family. Tommy couldn't stop weeping during the bible study. At the end of the meeting, he received prayer and gave his life to Jesus.

Tommy finally had peace in his heart. He began to make better choices. He threw away those expensive cigars. He stopped drinking and started living right. He was set free by the power of God. Today, Tommy is reunited with his children. He never remarried because he is content being single. He is happy just fellowshipping with the Holy Spirit. Tommy sometimes travels with the pastor and drives him to different speaking engagements. Tommy is no longer depressed. He is set free. If you have an addiction that needs to be broken, Jesus can break it.

Dear Heavenly Father,

I come to you humbly as I know how. I confess that I have an addiction of _____ and I need deliverance today. I repent of my sins. Wash me in your blood today and make me whole. I can't live bound anymore. I am tired of sinning against you. I decree that Jesus lives on the throne of my heart. Heal me Lord and set me free. Thank you for answering this prayer in Jesus' name. Amen.

CHAPTER TWO

Adultery

BY YOLANDA SAMUEL

Did you know that adultery destroys lives? Did you know it is a sin that is based on selfishness and deception? According to Merriam-Webster, adultery is sex between a married person and someone who is not that person's wife or husband.[4] Proverbs 6:32 says, "But whoso committeth adultery with a woman lacketh understanding: he that doeth it destroyeth his own soul." Being involved in adultery dulled my conscious, and eventually, I started feeling justified in doing the act. I have witnessed the destruction of infidelity in my life. I was deceived into believing I was making his life better by being what his wife wasn't. I could never be his wife. Adultery had me bound and blind to sin. Adultery cost me everything!

CONSEQUENCES

Now that we know what adultery is let's discuss some of its consequences. If we don't get ahold of adultery and receive deliverance, it will cost us the following:

1. Lies

Proverbs 19:5 says, "A false witness shall not go unpunished, and he who that speaketh lies shall not escape." I had to lie to live this lifestyle continually. I didn't go unpunished. Once you tell one lie, you must continue lying. For us to see each other, he had to lie to his wife. There were times we created lies together. Eventually, I lost track of all the lies I told. Lies are based on selfishness. It was all about us, and what we wanted to do. When we agreed to lie, we decided to walk in deception.

One example of lying is in (Acts 5:1-1) the story of Ananias and Sapphira who were husband and wife. The early church in the book of Acts was on one accord in heart and mind. It was agreed that they all would share their possessions, so the money could be distributed among everyone as it was needed. They decided in their hearts to lie and hold back a portion of the money for themselves. Not only did they lie to Peter, but they also lied to God and the Holy Spirit. When they laid the money at Peter's feet, he discerned they were not honest. He told them the devil filled their hearts to lie to the Holy Spirit (Acts 5:3). Having a clean heart in this church was important. Lying resulted in both of their deaths. Therefore, we must walk in truth.

2. Pride

Proverbs 29:23 says, "A man's pride shall bring him low, but honour shall uphold the humble in spirit." I was at my lowest because my pride had me blind to my wrongdoing. Many who are in adultery feel like it's alright for them to get their needs met outside of their husband or wife. Pride is the very nature of Satan. Job 41:34 says, "He beholdeth all high things; he is king over all the children of pride." A spirit of pride makes it all about us. We feel, we have arrived, and can't fall. Therefore, this sin is so dangerous.

One example of pride is Naaman in 2 Kings 5:11. He was a captain of the host of the king of Syria. He was a mighty and brave man but suffered from leprosy. The Syrians went out and raided the land of Israel and captured a young maid. She suggested to Naaman's wife that he go to Israel to see the prophet who could heal him. The king of Syria sent a letter to inform the king of Israel that Naaman was coming to see him to cure him of this disease. When Naaman came to Elisha's house, and he stood at his door. Elisha sent a messenger to tell Naaman to wash in the Jordan River seven times so that he can be healed. Naaman became angry and thought Elisha should come to him in person. He felt he was too important to wash in the river in Israel because the rivers of Damascus were better. He also felt that Elisha should have healed him in a way that would take less effort on his part. As a result of his pride, he almost lost out on his healing. After he humbled himself, listened to his servants, and followed his instructions, he was healed.

3. Betrayal

Philippians 2:3 says, "Let nothing be done through strife or vainglory; conceit, but in lowliness of mind let each esteem other better than themselves." Selfishness is a dangerous sin. I was selfish and only thought about what the situation did for me. He only told me his view of the marriage, so in my eyes, he was the victim. He betrayed his wife, and I betrayed God by participating in this sin. Betraying is when someone violates that person's trust. Once a person is betrayed, they lose trust in the person who betrayed them.

One example of betrayal is Judas Iscariot's betrayal of Jesus. He was one of Jesus' twelve disciples. Jesus knew Judas' heart had begun to stray from him. He was with Jesus for three years! He saw, the miracles and heard his sermons, yet he had greed in his heart. His relationship with Jesus was not real. He oversaw the money and was a thief. He took what he needed as he saw fit. Luke 22:3-4 says, "Then entered Satan into Judas surnamed Iscariot, being the number of the twelve. And he went his way, and communed with the chief priests and captains, how he might betray him to them." There was an open door in his life for the enemy to use him. Satan tried to stop Jesus from going to the cross to sacrifice his life for our sins. In the Garden of Gethsemane, he led the authorities to Jesus. He showed his betrayal by kissing Jesus on the cheek. Money and power were his gods. He thought it would benefit him to betray Jesus. This betrayal brought shame and guilt, and he took his own life as a result of realizing the magnitude of the sin he committed.

4. Lust

Timothy 2:22 says, "Flee youthful passions lusts: but follow righteousness, faith, charity, peace, with them that call on the Lord out of a pure heart." I had lust in my heart. That was the very sin, that connected me to this married man. Instead of running away, I ran right into sin. My lust was never satisfied because it had to be fed daily. This lust we had for each other was purely physical and felt like it was real love. Lust is a strong desire to have or do something that may not be good for us. It is usually flesh based. If lust is in your heart, you will be tempted to satisfy the longings of your flesh when temptations are presented to you.

One example of lust is the story of Samson in Judges 16. Sampson was Israel's God appointed judge and was to be a Nazarite. Samson had superhuman strength. The Angel of the Lord visited his mother and was warned never to eat anything that comes from a vine, drink no wine, or eat anything unclean (Judges 13:13-14). He was also told not to cut his hair. Sampson's lists caused him to break these vows. He made terrible choices concerning women. He was involved with Philistine women. One of those women contributed to his downfall. Delilah was a harlot and was offered money to find out the secret to Samson's strength so that they could capture him. She tortured him daily to tell her his secret to his strength. He tricked her a few times, then finally he gave in and told her if his hair is cut, it makes him weak. He laid in her lap one evening to take a nap, and she cut his hair off. He was captured by the Philistines, had his eyes removed, and put in prison. God used Samson to destroy more

Philistines during his death than He did throughout his life. His lust for wayward women costs his anointing and life. I will tell you the story of how adultery cost me everything!

YOLANDA'S TESTIMONY

I was exposed to adultery as a teenager. I saw the impact it has on a persons' self-esteem and marriage. I vowed as I got older, never to be in an adulterous relationship. When we say things like, "I'll never do what my mom or dad did," it is a form of judgment. I judged them based on what I saw. Luke 6:37 says, "Judge not, and ye shall not be judged: condemn not, and ye shall be condemned: forgive, and ye shall be forgiven." I was so busy judging that I didn't see my mess. I saw how it hurt my mom's marriage. I spent most of my adult life, being angry at my dad because of it. Proverbs 28:26 says," He that trusteth in his own heart is a fool: but whoso walketh wisely, he shall be delivered." Little did I know I would need deliverance in the future.

At 19 years old, I decided to join the United States Navy. I wasn't ready for the discipline of college. I felt my parents were strict, and I was ready to do all the things they never allowed my sister and I to do. I was engaged to an older guy at 17. He was a few years older than me, and my mom wasn't happy about the situation. I was in love, and that was all that mattered. We dated for about two years. My mom is very sensitive spiritually. She knew he wasn't the one for me. I had plans to be with him, but Proverbs 19:21 states, "There are many devices in a man's heart; nevertheless the counsel of the Lord, that shall stand." I was raised in the church and knew right from wrong. While I was in boot camp, my fiancé wrote me and ended our relationship. It was devastating for me. After the breakup, I was ready to live the life of a young woman without having to hide or sneak around. The enemy had a trap waiting on me.

It felt good to be a young adult and being able to come and go as I pleased after basic training. I became promiscuous during that time. I began drinking and partying. That was only the beginning. James 1:15 says, "Then when lust hath conceived, it bringeth forth sin: and sin, when it is finished, bringeth forth death." The lust I began to feed became sin that caused my life to change. I was stationed at my second duty station in 1997 in Norfolk, Virginia. I was excited to go to a new command. I was 22 years old, ready to meet new people and have some fun. I had no idea, the trap the enemy had for me. 1 Peter 5:8 says, "Be sober, be vigilant; because your adversary the devil prowls around like a roaring lion, looking for someone to devour." I would soon be entrapped in a relationship, that was hard to get out of.

When I first saw him, I was immediately attracted to him. He was tall, light-skinned, muscular built with hazel eyes. I was the new girl on the block, so I already knew guys would be after me. We met on the mess decks (eating area), and we hit it off immediately. He also found me attractive. He got married as a teenager right after basic training. I was okay with that because I only planned to be his friend. He had other plans. James 1:14 says, "But every man is tempted, when he is drawn away of his own lusts, and enticed." Our lust of the flesh is what drew us to each other.

As time went on, we got to know each other, and our feelings began to grow. We talked every day. Back then, we had pagers. He would page me, and I would call him after working hours. We would meet out in town without our friends so we could get some time together away from everyone. There was this guy in the Airforce that I was dating. He was nice but boring to me. He seemed too laid back, a clean cut, and I liked bad boys. He picked me up on a Saturday so we could spend the day together. All he did was play video games while I sat and watched. I was bored and was thinking about my friend. So, I got one of my friends to page me. I lied and said that I had to go back to the ship for an emergency. Proverbs 19:5 says, "A false witness shall not be un punished, and he that speaketh lies shall not escape." Adultery is based on lies. That became the foundation of our illegal relationship. As soon as the guy dropped me off, the married guy and I went to a hotel and had sex for the first time. The word says in Proverbs 22:14 "The mouth of strange women is a deep pit: he that is abhorred of the LORD shall fall therein." I said and did whatever it took to be with him.

We were going strong for a few months. We became even bolder and went out to a restaurant to eat. I was hoping we didn't run into anyone I knew. Every weekend, we were at the hotel, I paid for the room every time. We were telling each other we loved each other. My feelings grew even more. He got in trouble and ended up being on restriction which meant he could not leave the ship at all for a certain amount of days. I would smuggle alcohol to him and others who were restricted. One day, I went up to get some food, and his wife was visiting him. My heart dropped. "What was she doing here?" I thought. I was better than her and better for him from what he told me. He told me what I wanted to hear. I found out that he was bold with the previous women he slept with. He would invite them to their house when he had cookouts! He was used to getting the women with his flattering words, Psalms 55:21 says, "The words of his mouth were smoother than butter, but war was in his heart: his words were softer than oil, yet were they drawn swords." Those words were laced with deception.

Some of my friends began to tell me of all the women he was with previously. Some I hung out with unknowingly. I was angry and embarrassed. I had no idea he was a player like that. I thought I was different and special. He eventually stayed in trouble and ended up getting kicked out of the military. One evening, I was at our usual meeting spot or the hotel waiting for him to arrive. When he got there, I could feel something wasn't right. He then told me. He was starting to feel guilty about cheating because his wife was pregnant with their first child. I tried to convince him. This was different from his other flings because we loved each other, but he had his mind made up. Galatians 6:7 says, "Be not deceived; God is not mocked: for whatsoever a man soweth, that shall he also reap." That time had finally come for me.

Some weeks passed, and I was devastated. He was out of the military, and we were getting ready to go on a six-month deployment. How would I ever get over him? I stayed celibate for almost a year and didn't date for nearly that long. After we returned from the deployment, he came to see me. I then saw his baby daughter. He said he missed me, but I knew I couldn't get tangled in that web again. Galatians 5:1 says, "Stand fast therefore in the liberty wherewith Christ hath made us free, and be not entangled again with the yoke of bondage." It took months to get over him, so I had to stay free. He told me he was moving back home to New Orleans with his family soon. I knew for sure it was over between us. The attraction and friendship we had were still there. It was based on lies and our lust. It wasn't real, even though it felt like it was. Lastly, we will see how God changed my life.

GOD'S REDEMPTIVE PLAN

Next, I got stationed in Tampa, Florida in 1997. There was an older woman who was a Christian in the Army. My life was a mess. I was drinking and still living wild. She never changed, she treated me like her own. She invited me to church with her. I went with her. That was the Sunday in November 1997, that I gave my life to Christ. I felt brand new. I came back to my barracks room and poured my alcohol down the sink. I was finally free. I found a great church and joined. I began to serve in different church auxiliaries. I even got married in 2001. That marriage ended in divorce after 12 years due to adultery.

Marriage is a covenant between a man and a woman, not a mistress. Ephesians 5:31 says, "For this cause shall a man leave his father and mother, and shall be joined to his wife, and they two shall be one flesh." I was destroying a covenant. Praise God in 1997, I finally surrendered my life to Christ, and He freed me from that! I had to forgive myself and ask God to forgive me.

I learned, during my journey that adultery is not hard to get into. You don't have to be a low-down dirty person, to get caught up in it. A life void of Christ is a sure open door for the enemy. One thing for sure, I ended up being hurt from adultery in my previous marriage. He left me because he had strong feelings for another woman and divorced me. I ended up homeless and lost my car. That pain was unbearable! The Lord reminded me, that even though I repented, I still had those seeds in the ground that produced a harvest.

We often don't think about the consequences of our actions. I wasn't thinking about how his wife would feel if she knew about me. It was all about my pride and me. I believed the lies he told me because it felt so good at the time and we felt justified. I thank God I learned the truth. John 8:32 says, "And ye shall know the truth, and the truth shall make you free." It took time for Jesus to break that soul tie off my life. That is why sex is for marriage. A wife becomes one flesh with her husband (Matthew 19:5). Sex is a powerful act, and spirits are picked up from the person we join our body with.

Finally, I have learned that sin is nothing to play with. I threw away everything I knew was right, to do what I wanted. I thank God for my new chance at marriage and the victory I have in Him. You can be free today if you desire. God had a purpose and a plan for me. Jeremiah 29:11 says, "For I know the thoughts I think towards you, saith the LORD, thoughts of peace, and not of evil, to give you an expected end." He also has a plan for your life. Don't go on your path, stay connected to His! Don't allow the enemy to detour your destiny!

Dear Heavenly Father,

I come before You; I confess I am full of lies, pride, and lust. I need Your help to be free. 1 John 2:16 says, "For all, that is in the world, the lust of the flesh, the lust of the eyes, and the pride of life, is not of the Father, but is of the world." I ask that You forgive me of these sins and close any open doors in my life. Help me to fill my Spirit full of Your word, so that I will not follow what my flesh desires. I ask that You reveal and destroy the root causes of how this sin came into my life. I ask for You to wash me clean of all unrighteousness, and uproot selfishness, lies, and rebellion out of my heart. I desire to stay pure, for my future wife or future husband. I thank You, for forgiving me. I choose this day to stay free with Your power, which lives in me. Because I have confessed my sin, You are faithful and just to forgive me and cleanse me of all unrighteousness (1 John 1:9). Thank You for forgiving me. I ask You to walk me through this deliverance process in Jesus' name that I pray. Amen.

CHAPTER THREE
Alcoholism

BY CORETTA KELSEY

Unfortunately, alcohol has caused major issues in families. People who drink alcohol sometimes engage in violent behavior. Alcohol can even become deadly when too much is consumed resulting in alcohol poisoning. According to Merriam-Webster, alcoholism has been one of the most damaging addictions.[5] It has been typically characterized by the inability to control alcoholic drinking, impairment of the ability to work and socialize. As a child, I lived through alcohol addiction. By the Grace of God, I am here to tell my story. It almost took me out several times. Growing up with alcoholism cost me everything! Proverbs 20:1 says, "Wine is a mocker, strong drink is raging: and whosoever is deceived thereby is not wise."

CONSEQUENCES

Now that we have discussed what alcoholism is let me share some of the consequences. If we don't help our loved ones with their addiction and pray for their deliverance, it will cost us the following:

1. Chaos in The Home

If you are an alcoholic or have an alcoholic in your home, please seek help. If you are the parent that is the alcoholic, stop and think about the effect that it has on your children. Alcohol will cause you to act or behave like an entirely different person. If you could view yourself from the eyes of others, you would probably never take another drink in your life. An alcoholic is not able to respond logically, drive, cook or sometimes even walk. Alcoholics can become abusive and be a danger to themselves as well as others.

2. Spirit of Rejection

Unfortunately, the spirit of rejection enters the victims of the abuser as well as their loved ones. When I was very young, I felt rejection from my mother since she had no control of her drinking problem. I would talk to God and ask why he allowed me to be born to someone that hated me and abused me. If I didn't feel the love from my parents, of course, I would feel rejection from everyone that I met. It was instilled in me from a young age. I would always look in the mirror to question why I was not accepted. Why wasn't I good enough? I never saw any promising future for me. I just knew that I had nothing to look forward to in life. The spirit of rejection kept me depressed, afraid and bound. Timothy 1:7 says, "For God has not given us the spirit of fear; but power, and love and sound mind." Jeremiah 29:11 says, "For I know the thoughts that I think towards you, saith the Lord, thoughts of peace, and not of evil, to give you an expected end."

3. Resentment/Behavioral Issues

I had to make myself feel better by standing up to people who made fun of my mom for being an alcoholic. When my friends would tease me about my mom being drunk, I would get so mad. I would be ready to fight. Living in a small town didn't help. I remember us being at the liquor store before it opened in the mornings. I would be so ashamed which made me start behaving poorly in school. I had no one to push me about my grades or anything. I didn't care about life at this point anymore! My mom began to call me all kinds of names and whipped us for whatever reason just because she was drunk. I just wanted out! I continued to ask God why I had to suffer. I promised myself that I would never put my children through such embarrassment. 2 Chronicles 7:14 says, "If my people, which are called by my name, shall humble themselves, and pray, and seek my face, and turn from their wicked ways; then will I hear from heaven, and forgive their sins, and will heal their land."

Noah is an example of someone that became so drunk that he fell asleep. His sons saw him this way and covered him up (Genesis 9:21-23). Who wants to see their parents in this state?

Another story I would like to touch on is how Lot's daughters gave him too much wine on purpose so that they could sleep with him and become pregnant (Genesis 19:32-38). You must be aware of your surroundings because people can take advantage of you when you are drunk. Most alcoholics recall very little of what took place while they were in their drunken state. Alcoholism can lead to rape, abuse and so many other things!

4. Low Self Esteem

Does she love me? What is love? Is this what God brought me into as a child? The lady that gave birth to me hates me! What did I do to deserve this? Why am I continually being punished by her? We ran into several ditches while she drove us after or during drinking. I was abused verbally, physically and mentally. Who does this to their children? I didn't like her. I didn't want her to be my mom. My cousins' mothers treat them well. Why doesn't my dad know that we need out of here? I smelled the alcohol and smoke daily. It was so embarrassing! We were at the liquor store early in the morning waiting for them to open! I always hope that none of my friends would see us there before breakfast time.

Who tells their child to get in a closet, covers them up with clothes and other things to hide them from everyone, to pretend that the child ran away? Who does this kind of stuff to a kid? I was threatened not to say a word. I had to stay in the closet for hours while she called all the family and close friends. She lied and said I had run away! What did I do to be treated that way? This was not right at all! Later I found out that my mother did all of this to make my dad feel bad. She wanted him to feel guilty because he wasn't home for a few hours. Alcohol made my life a living hell!

CORETTA'S TESTIMONY

There were times I questioned why I was born? Why would God give me to an alcoholic mom and a father who never said he loved me? I don't remember hearing that from either parent growing up. I did, however, inherit their work ethics. They were both very hard workers. My mom is an excellent cook, always has been. The only thing she would allow me to do is clean the house and make hot water cornbread. My parents never took us to the movies or anything. Maybe they couldn't afford it, but they always indulged in their habits or wants. My dad was a marijuana smoker and used alcohol occasionally. My parents love me, and I know this now. I understand that parents are not perfect, and I did not realize this until I became one. I made plenty of mistakes as a parent, but one thing I consistently do is tell my children that I love them.

GODS REDEMPTION

Once God gave me an understanding of why my mom became an alcoholic, it made me have compassion for her. I even considered her becoming a mother at the age of nineteen years old. She did not enjoy life or have a mom that was alive to guide her. She had no one to explain to her how to be a parent. It has taken me years to have compassion on her. When God had me to pray for her despite how she brought me up, he answered my prayers.

He delivered her from her addiction. She was even able to give up cigarettes as well. God has blessed her. She now has a hunger for God and is trying her best to live right. My mother received the Holy Spirit with the evidence of speaking in tongues. She has even had visitations from the Lord. God is a God that holds true to His promise. John 14:13 says, "And whatsoever ye shall ask in my name, that will I do, that the Father may be glorified in the son."

Dear Heavenly Father,

I come to you to confess of my sins that I have allowed to take root in me. I am full of bitterness and un-forgiveness. I also have trust issues due to the way I was brought up dealing with alcoholism and the abuse from it. I need You to set me free from these strongholds Jesus! Please break every chain and tear down all these walls that have gone up in my life. I need you to deliver me from the pain and the hurt. Deliver me from these sins. Make me over again! I need You to help me to forgive completely and to love as You do, Christ Jesus! Help me to trust those that love me. Help me to forgive those that have hurt me. These sins will no longer bind me! I am free because of you Jesus. I am free! Hallelujah! Amen.

CHAPTER FOUR

Anger

BY ANGELA RICHARDSON

Anger is an emotion that has been associated with the element of fire. Have you ever heard the term "hot head?" Anger can be controlled by applying the Word of God and then walking in the fruit of self-control. However, from time to time, anger has a way of manifesting in our lives in the most stressful instances.[6] The spirit of anger will cost you everything if you don't get it under control. Anger has destroyed many marriages, families, relationships, jobs and many other things because the person who was dealing with it didn't seek help. They were always blaming everyone else for their behavior, instead of owning up to the problem. You must first admit that you have a problem before you can get help for it. Denial is not good. It can't always be everyone else's fault all the time in every situation of your life.[6]

According to Merriam Webster, anger is a strong feeling of displeasure and usually antagonism (opposition of a conflicting force, tendency, principle).[7] Ephesians 4:31-32 (AMP) says, "Let all bitterness and indignation and wrath (passion, rage, bad temper) and resentment (anger, animosity) and quarreling (brawling, clamor, contention), and slander (evil speaking, abusive or blasphemous language) be banished from you with all malice(spite, ill will). And become useful and helpful and kind to one another, tenderhearted (compassionate, understanding, loving heart) forgiving one another (readily and freely) as God in Christ forgave you."

Have you let the spirit of anger stop you from moving forward in life? Learn to start forgiving others for offending or hurting you in the past. Have you allowed the spirit of anger to affect you and all your relationships? A study published in the journal Behavioral Science & Law states that, "9% of American adults or about 22 million people have a history of impulse angry behavior and have access to at least one gun. About 1.5% of people about 3.7 million people with impulse anger issues carry guns around with them when they are outside of their homes." The adults in this study admitted that they lose their temper to the point of having uncontrollable "tantrums" which sometimes includes breaking or smashing things and getting into physical fights.[8]

CONSEQUENCES

Anger is a spiritual problem that must be dealt with, so we can live peaceful lives with our spouses, families, friends, co-workers and whoever that we may meet in our lives. Romans 12:18 (Amp) says, "If possible as far as it depends on you, live at peace with everyone." Are you ready to move forward from always getting angry at everything and everybody to living a peaceful life on this earth? Anger is a destiny stopping spirit that must be broken. Now that we have seen some of the statistics that comes from not dealing with uncontrollable anger let us look now at some of the consequences that will arise if we don't get a handle on this emotion. Here are several implications that will occur: sickness in the body, unforgiveness, bad attitude, retaliation, grudges, and frustration.

1. Sickness or diseases affecting your body

Proverbs 17:22 (AMP) says, "A happy heart is good medicine and a joyful mind causes healing, But a broken spirit dries up the bones." This scripture means that a joyful heart doesn't bring on sickness or disease but a broken (hurt, angry) spirit dries up the bones and you start having health issues like back issues, spinal problems, bone issues, and many other health issues that don't have a known origin. When your mind is shattered and not working correctly (healthy), then you will see symptoms developing in your body most of the time. If the doctor can't find a medical diagnosis for your symptoms, then we must do a heart search to see when the symptoms started. So, we will know who we need to forgive and how to begin managing our anger with the Word of God so the Word can transform us.

2. Unforgiveness

Colossians 3:13 (AMP) says, "Bearing graciously with one another, and willingly forgiving each other if one has a cause for complaint against another; just as the Lord has forgiven you, so should you forgive." God is very serious about us forgiving one another. Forgiveness is mentioned throughout the Old Testament and New Testament. I have seen many people from all races and nationalities let anger control their responses in certain situations that they encounter in life. Uncontrolled anger is the number one cause of murders in the world today. Anger is a clear indicator that someone is holding on to an offense. Unforgiveness separates us from the presence of God. Unforgiveness will lead you to a spiritually dry place. When people are accustomed to feeling God's love and presence, they often feel lost when they're unable to sense Him. They don't realize that they may be feeling disconnected from God's presence because they are refusing to forgive. Forgiveness is an act of will. Once forgiveness and restoration of mind, body, and spirit have occurred, love, joy, and gratitude for all things that He has done will come flooding in.[9]

3. Bad Attitudes

Proverbs 4:23-24 (AMP) says, "Watch over your heart will all diligence, for from it flow the springs of life. Put from you a deceitful (lying, misleading mouth), And put devious lips from you." A bad attitude will not get you anywhere in life. When you always walk around with an angry scowl on your face, many people avoid you and retreat the other way. When all wounds are healed, you will walk around with a smile on your face, and a pep in your step with joy, peace, and freedom in the Holy Ghost. Problems and issues may come into your life but when you are walking in the peace of God things don't bother you as they use too.

4. Retaliation

Romans 12:19 (AMP) says, "Beloved, never avenge yourselves, but leave the way open for God's wrath (and His judicial righteousness); for it is written (in scripture), "Vengeance is mine, I will repay," says the Lord." We are not to try to get the person back that has hurt you, but we are to pray and let God handle the situation the way He wants to handle it. Majority of the time if we try to handle it, we will make a mess of things. Just pray and wait on the solution from God on all issues that you are going through in life.

5. Grudges

Ephesians 4:2-3 (AMPC) says, "Living as becomes you with complete lowliness of mind (humility) and meekness (unselfishness), gentleness, mildness) with patience bearing with one another and making allowances because we love one another. Be eager and strive earnestly to guard and keep the harmony and oneness of (and produced by) the Spirit in binding power of peace." This scripture talks about forgiveness, and we are to forgive people instead of holding grudges against them for the wrong things that they have done to us. We are not to hold other people's short coming against them because we have had many short comings in our lives as well. We wouldn't always want to be reminded of what we did and didn't do, so we must not hold what they do against them. Stop bringing things back up that we said that we have already forgiven them for. Because if we have truly forgiven them of it, there is no reason to bring it back up when we get mad at them. We are all flawed human beings, but by the grace of God, we can overcome anything with His help.

6. Frustration

Philippians 4:7 (AMP) says, "And the peace of God (that peace which reassures the heart, that peace) which transcends all understanding (that peace which) stand guard over your hearts and your minds in Christ Jesus (is yours)." We don't have anything to be frustrated about if we would give the situation over to God and leave it there. We would be much better off. We will start walking in a peace that surpasses all understanding, and this kind of peace can only come from God. We are to pray to God about everything no matter what it is. Nothing is too small to pray and ask God about. Don't let anyone or anything take your peace from you. Situations will arise in our lives but let God work it out. Sometimes we try to work it out by ourselves, but our strength is limited. God has unlimited power to move mountains that seem too high for us to go over or around. Pray and give it to Jesus and wait. When it doesn't look like God is moving, He is. God does all His work in the background. Just know that if God said it, then it will come to pass in our lives. God cannot lie. It will happen when we least expect it. We are to always pray for God's will to be done in our lives. He wants the best for us and knows what is best for us. So, go to bed and go to sleep. Rest assured that He has everything that concerns you under control.

ANGELA'S TESTIMONY

Now that we have covered the consequences of anger let me tell you how it nearly cost me everything. I had to let the spirit of anger go before it consumed me and stopped my destiny. Anger cost me relationships with my family and friends. It stole my peace. I was always doing things for other people, family, friends, but never investing in myself. Taking people to their doctor appointments was taking care of everyone one else's needs before my own needs. I was pulled this way and that way. I never seemed to get my needs met. I was walking around existing, but not living. I tend to over analyze everything and worry about things that I have no control over. I have been in stressful situations. I laid in bed many nights not able to sleep because I was trying to figure out things on my own. I ended up taking sleeping pills to help me to sleep at night. They helped me sleep most of the time if I could get my mind to shut down and relax. I used to go to sleep and wake up the next morning feeling like I haven't even slept that night. It is hard to go about your day when you wake up tired. I was worrying and staying awake many nights even after taking medicine. I cried out to God telling Him that, "I needed help." If I didn't get it, I was going to explode and maybe do something that I might regret the rest of my life. I needed to start investing in my sanity.

So, I heard on Periscope a teaching by Lajun and Valora Cole. Valora stated that she would be starting a mentorship program. So, I called my husband and talked to him about it. He agreed with me taking the class, so I signed up, and the rest is history.

The mentorship helped me deal with a lot of things. The first class was about "Healing of the Wounded Soul." It spoke to me. I had been dealing with anger for a long time. Something that happened to me when I was a child had caused me to be angry. I remember I always walking around with a serious face because of the pain that I was feeling. All the way back to my childhood I can remember that I lived in a dysfunctional family. My dad had an alcohol problem. I remember on Fridays he would get paid. Instead of bringing his money home to our family, he would get dropped off at a club in my home town.

Whenever he made it home, he was sloppy drunk. Most of his money was already gone. I remember there were times that our utilities were cut off. He spent more money and time at that little club than he did at home. When I was twelve or thirteen years old, he left one day and never came back. My mom didn't know where to find him. I must admit the house was much more peaceful after he left. I felt rejected and abandoned by my father. My mom was able to get a job at one of the local motels. She was able to get us on food stamps so we could eat. I thank God for my grandmother who lived next door to us at the time. She helped us with the bills until my mom could get her a job. My mom had to get the utilities paid up so nothing would get cut off. I remember getting ready to graduate from High School. I went to my dad. I was excited to tell him that I was going to graduate and invited him to attend. He made every excuse not to come to my graduation, and he didn't show up.

I married a young man I knew in school, and we moved to another city. He became abusive and got drunk all the time. I

It Cost Me Everything

stayed in that marriage for a long time. By the grace of God, I moved back home and got a divorce. My next marriage wasn't too much better. My husband was jealous and took it out on me physically and mentally. I was trying to go to Practical Nursing School. I worked part-time on 3-11 shifts at the hospital. I started praying and asking God to get me out of that abusive situation. He did. I left there, and a month later he married again. These are some of the things that happened to me over the years that caused me to harbor anger in my life. At the time, I never dealt with all that anger. I married again in 2009. He is so sweet, caring and loves God which is the most crucial aspect of our marriage. I injured my back at a nursing home in 2011. I was in pain all the time and was unable to work a job. God has brought us through as we continued to depend on and trust Him. Other things have happened over the years to add fuel to the fire. My Dad and I reconciled. In 2015 he passed. I was able to lead him to the Lord before he left this earth.

GOD'S REDEMPTION

All the pent-up anger was released the night of the first mentorship class. The first class we had was "Healing of the Wounded Soul," and I received deliverance. I started the prayer line at 6 am and 12 pm every day with Prophetess Kimberly Moses. It has helped me to grow closer to God. We are praying at 6 am for an hour in tongues. She teaches and encourages us to move forward in God. Sometimes you need someone to speak positive things into your life by letting you know that God loves and cares all about you. God is concerned about the things that you are concerned about. Also, Prophetess Kimberly

Moses gives us scriptures to meditate on. Be rest assured that God wants all of us to succeed in all that we do. I have felt so empowered since starting the mentorship as well as the prayer line. God is moving so much in my life right now. Some of it is unexplainable. God knows for sure what I need and when I need it. Philippians 4:19 (AMP) says, "And my God will liberally supply (fill until full) your every need according to His riches in glory in Christ Jesus."

God is so concerned that I received healing on the prayer line at 6 am one morning. I had called the prayer line wanting prayer for one of my legs being longer than the other one. My right leg was shorter than my left leg, so I was having problems because I was staggering, falling, and had pain in both of my hips due to one leg being shorter than the other one. So, I asked for prayer that morning, and Prophetess Kimberly told me to sit on the couch with my legs stretched out on the sofa. They began to pray, and I watched my right leg move down toward the left leg. I got up and walked around. My leg felt great. I touched my right hip, and the pain was gone. But when I touched the left hip there was still pain, so they prayed again. Prophetess Kimberly stated, "The Lord said that you would continue to get better with the hip pain." I already had a scheduled appointment with the podiatrist the next day, so I went to my appointment. The doctor came in and put a mark on both of my ankles. The mark was in the inside of my feet. As he put my feet together, he said, "That he couldn't tell the difference between the two legs and that my feet were matching up. I told the doctor that, "I had called the prayer line that morning and I got healed after prayer.

I have been on the prayer line ever since. If I oversleep, my husband will wake me up to make sure that I get on the line.

I feel the joy of the Lord. I have gotten off some of the medication that I was taking before starting the mentorship and prayer line. By the end of November, I have gotten off the medication that I was taking for nerve pain. I took it for three years, but I don't need it any longer. Since December 2018, I have stopped taking even more medication including the pills that helped me sleep. I don't need it anymore, because I have the peace of God. I have released and forgiven all the people that have hurt or disappointed me in the past. I asked God to please bring back to my remembrance anybody that I still needed to forgive so that I can forgive them. I go throughout the day saying to myself, "I am an overcomer. I put on the full armor of Christ." I know that God is doing a great work in me. I have laid down my will for His will. I know that if we are living on this earth, other things will come up, but I refuse to let it stop me from moving forward.

In Luke 17:1-4 (AMP) says, "Jesus said to His disciples Stumbling blocks (temptations and traps set to lure one to sin) are sure to come, but woe (judgment is coming) to him through whom they come!" "It would be better for him if a milestone (as large as one turned by a donkey) were hung around his neck and he were hurled in the sea, than for him to cause one of these little ones to stumble (in sin and lose faith)." "Pay attention and always be on guard (looking out for one another)!" "If your brother sins and disregards God's precepts, solemnly warn him; and if he repents and changes, forgive him. "Even if he sins against you seven times and says, "I repent; you must forgive him (that is given up resentment and consider offense recalled and annulled)."

We must resist the bait of the enemy, Satan. He comes to steal, kill and destroy our lives. I know that many people can identify with the spirit of anger, but it is time to get healed and set free of this emotion that is controlling you. We will be able to walk in the freedom that only God can give us. God loves us so much that He doesn't want to leave us broken and shattered in our emotions. God has set me free from these old wounds, hurts, and disappointments that have happened up to this present time in my life. It hasn't been easy to forgive, but by the grace of God, I know for me to walk in peace, I must forgive and move on with my life. Stop letting anger hold you hostage. Use your faith to activate God's grace. His grace is sufficient for each one of us if we apply it to our lives. His strength will make us strong through our weakness. We can rely on God to help us through all the things that we may come up against in our lives.

Dear Heavenly Father,

I come before You today asking that You help me remove this spirit of anger that is trying to consume my life in Jesus' name. Lord, help me to be able to forgive everyone that has ever hurt me or disappointed me in my childhood up until this present time. I repent for letting the devil use me to take the bait of the offense and not walk in forgiveness in Jesus' name. Lord, You said in, Matthew 6:12 (AMP), "And forgive us our debts, as we forgive our debtors (letting go of both the wrong and the resentment)." Help me to release, bitterness, resentment, retaliation, bad attitudes, unforgiveness, and frustrations so there won't be any sicknesses or diseases that may try to attach itself to my body in Jesus' name. Lord, You said in Psalms 91:10 (AMPC), "There shall no evil befall you, nor any plague or calamity come near your tent." Lord, I realize that forgiving the person of the offense will help me walk closer to You in Jesus' name. Lord, I veto and cancel all anger in my life and all the consequences that come with it in Jesus' name. I speak life into me right now. I will live and not die and declare the works of the Lord in Christ Jesus. I will move forward in the things of God in Jesus' name. I will walk in freedom, joy, peace, and love in every area of my life from this day forward. I will rest in Your presence and lay all my trials and disappointments at Your feet for You to handle in Jesus' name. Amen.

CHAPTER FIVE
Depression

BY JENNIFER JACKSON

Have you ever wondered why depression is commonly known as a mood disorder and effects so many people in different ways? There are various people called by God from Moses, David, Hannah, Elijah and others who have battled with some form of depression while serving the Lord. Subsequently, now you see that even individuals in the Bible struggled with depression. According to Merriam-Webster, depression can be defined as a mood disorder inactivity, difficulty in thinking and concentration, a significant increase or decrease in appetite and time spent sleeping, feelings of dejection and hopelessness, and sometimes suicidal tendencies.[10] Jeremiah 20:18 (NLT) says, "Why was I ever born? My entire life has been filled with trouble sorrow and shame." Ten percent of American adults suffer from depression, and more than 38,000 people die by suicide each year.[11] Depression can be looked at has one of those silent killers that you never knew anyone was suffering from until you read that person's last words. I was once a part of that ten percent and it almost cost me everything.

CONSEQUENCES

Now that we understand why depression is called a mood disorder and its effects on so many people let's discuss some of its consequences. Depression leads to the following: loss of identity, suicidal thoughts and actions, isolation, hopelessness and being out of fellowship with God. These are some of the tactics used by the enemy to keep people bound from receiving the help and deliverance they need. As defined in Merriam-Webster a tactic is a device for accomplishing an end, a method of employing forces in combat.[12]

1. Loss of one's identity to the world

Romans 12:2 (NLT) says, "Don't copy the behavior and customs of this world, but let God transform you into a new person by changing the way you think. Then you will learn to know God's will for you, which is good and pleasing and perfect." God is determined for us to know that our identity was created through Him and by Him (Genesis 1:27). Depression is contrary to focusing on our identity in Christ and who we are in Him. I have seen and know so many people who have lost their identity because they were so busy trying to live up to the "standard" of the world they fell in a place of self-loathing — trying to conform pages on magazine, social media platform trends and some even to the pressures put on them by their families. Ultimately, they became only a shell of who they thought they were.

2. Suicidal Thoughts and Actions

Too often we open a magazine, login into our favorite social media platform and various news outlet you hear about a famous music artist, fashion designer, world-renowned chef and even leaders in ministry both in the world and in our local area have taken their lives only to find out they were suffering from depression. Jonah 4:3 says, "Therefore now, O Lord, just take my life from me, for it is better for me to die than to live." God has purposed for us to be in this world and for us not allow the world to define who we are. Contemplating suicide is one of the tactics that the enemy will try and paint a picture of your present state that isn't true. He will make you feel as though no one cares, when (1 Peters 5:7) reminds us that we are to cast all our cares upon the Lord. I've known people who contemplated suicide, and the Lord told me to speak His Word over their lives and remind them He didn't call them into the world, only to have them take themselves out.

3. Isolation

There are times in our lives when we want to get away and be by ourselves to have a moment of peace and quietness which is normal. However, when isolation seems to become your refuge or hiding place regularly, that's not normal. This is a tactic where the enemy will have you thinking that people are against you or they're out to destroy your life, when in fact it's the enemy who is trying to destroy you. Ecclesiastes 4:9-10 says, "Two are better than one because they have a more satisfying return for their labor; for if [a]either of them falls, the one will lift up his companion. But woe to him who is alone when he falls and does not have another to lift him up."

Isolation will cause you to live in fear of the people who genuinely want to help you and give you the support you need. Isolation will even present a distorted picture of God's love for you to the point you will think that even God hates you. Ecclesiastes 4:12 says, "And though one can overpower him who is alone, two can resist him. A cord of three strands is not quickly broken." When you have the power of God the Father, God the Son and The Holy Spirit working on your behalf even the voice of the enemy will have to flee from you. We must resist the voice of the enemy going into a place of isolation that can take longer to get back.

4. Hopelessness

To be hopeless means that you have no expectation of anything good succeeding in your life. You look at things from a pessimistic state of mind without looking at the big picture of the many possibilities in your life, and this is contrary to the word of God. Being in a state of hopelessness is like walking around with a dark rain cloud following you everywhere just waiting for something negative to happen so that the rain drops fall. God never wants any of us to become discouraged to the point we want to throw our hands up. Psalms 42:11-12 (NLT) reminds us to encourage ourselves.

We must ask ourselves according to these scriptures: Why am I discouraged? Why is my heart so sad? I will put my hope in God! I will praise him again—my Savior. Now I am deeply discouraged, but I will remember you—even from distant Mount Hermon, the source of the Jordan, from the land of Mount Mizar. Life is only over when you keep telling yourself that because it's what the enemy would have you to believe, but Ecclesiastes 9:4 says, "There is hope only for the living. As they say, "It's better to be a live dog than a dead lion!"

5. Being out of fellowship with God

A relationship is one thing that God desires to have with us. He always desires to commune with us. He created us to be in fellowship with Him. John 15:16 (AMP) says, "You have not chosen Me, but I have chosen you and I have appointed and placed and purposefully planted you, so that you would go and bear fruit and keep on bearing, and that your fruit will remain and be lasting, so that whatever you ask of the Father in My name [as My representative] He may give to you."

When a person is in a state of depression, a trick of the enemy is to draw the person away from family, friends, ministry and most of all God. The enemy will use a decision that you made outside the will of God to plant a seed of condemnation. He will use words and even people to make you think that God no longer loves you. This is far from the truth. Jeremiah 29: 11 says, "The thoughts the Lord has towards you are good thoughts and not thoughts of evil."

God never desires to be out of fellowship with His creation and His children. Even during the fall of man, God was concerned why He couldn't find Adam and Eve for their regularly scheduled talks. It wasn't like them not to be in the midst of the garden. Genesis 3:9 says, "But the Lord God called to Adam, and said to him, "Where are you?" The fact that God called Adam by name reminds us of how important he was to Him. Although Adam and Eve sinned against God, He didn't forsake them even when they were led out of the garden. He took care of them. Depression would have you to think that God is finished with you after a fall. But contrary to words of the enemy God is saying, "I am here, I will never leave nor forsake you."

JENNIFER'S TESTIMONY

Now that we have covered the consequences of depression, let me tell you how it truly cost me everything. As a child growing up in foster care, I always wondered why my biological family didn't want me. I always knew the reason why I was in foster care and ultimately that wasn't a good enough reason for me. I was placed in an awesome foster home along with my baby brother, and we lacked for nothing. We were raised in the church which was a blessing. I was adopted into an awesome family with brothers, a sister, nieces, nephews and cousins, never treated differently, loved and accepted as if blood-related. I still grew-up always wondering what it was about me that I wasn't worth trying to keep. I grew up with behavioral issues, as well as having to receive counseling growing up. I grew up holding these feelings in of how much I hated myself.

My outlet was to eat and keep it all in, which also carried over into my adult life. I began to compare myself to other people and how people treated them. I would ask God, "Why was I brought into this world?" When I was sixteen years old, I was full of doubt and self-hatred to the point that the enemy had me so convinced that I didn't deserve to be in this world. I was depressed beyond the point of no return that went outside on the patio. I just broke down and said to God, "It's okay if you take my life tonight, I'm good without being in the world."

Even after I joined the military, I was still battling with depression. At this point, it was as if depression and I had a love-hate relationship. We would divorce one day and be reconciled another day. I was a functional depressant. I would walk around smiling wondering if anyone could see it. I needed someone to see that I was hurting. By this point, the enemy was giving me ways to take my life. I would get off from work and go back into my self-loathing state. My weight was fluctuating. I began to develop headaches all the while working and taking care of other people. Depression had hurt my relationship with certain people because instead of opening up I was too concerned that they would look at me differently. I was afraid that they wouldn't see me as a strong person. I was always sticking up for other people, but I wouldn't stand up for myself. Depression cost me everything!

GOD'S REDEMPTION

It wasn't until I got stationed in Kaiserslautern, Germany that I decided to listen to the voice of God. One thing I learned about God is that sometimes it takes moving you from a place you know for Him to get your attention. After getting back from my first deployment to Kuwait in 2007, reality set in with a lot of personal and family issues. Although they were heavy, I was still determined not to be moved and to trust God in the process. I remember going to the "Real Women's Conference" around 2008. A play was presented during a portion of the conference. During the play, there was praise dance to Kurt Carr's "I Almost Let Go." This song ministered to me because I was at a point that I wanted to give up. This song was speaking everything that I was feeling at that point. That's when I knew God was with me. He heard my prayer and words of confession during the conference. I was so ready to throw in the towel. The song reminded me that it was because of God that I am still here. He had never let me go regardless of what picture the enemy was painting. Following the conference, I grabbed hold of Psalms 139:13-14 (AMP), "For you have formed my innermost parts; You knit me (together) in my mother's womb. I will give thanks and praise to You, for I am fearfully and wonderfully made; Wonderful are Your works, and my soul knows it very well."

Through those scriptures, God reaffirmed to me that He validated me. I have a purpose because He brought me into this world. Yes, the enemy tried to come at me so many times with, "You know that's not true." I was determined that God's voice was louder than the enemy's. When the devil did come at me, I gave the Word back to him. I wasn't going to lose the momentum that God had pushed me into and go back to where He pulled me out of. I continued to stand on the Word of God no matter how hard it seemed. Although the enemy was trying to turn up the heat in my mind, I stood on 1 Thessalonian 2: 13. The word of God is the truth. Because His word is true, it will not return to Him void, I took a stand for myself. I no longer compared myself to other people. I was comfortable with who God said I was in Him. I remember reading Jeremiah 1:5. It hit me so hard like a stack of bricks that God knew me even before I was in my mother's womb. He called me out with purpose. I was truly settled in my mind.

Following my assignment to Germany, I was stationed in Fort Hood, TX (Killeen). God started to build me up in my prayer life, fasting and being in His Word. He placed me around great ministry leaders who challenged me to grow. That was something that I truly needed; accountability. People who wouldn't just let me wallow around but pushed me to grow in the things of God. God strategically started putting me in places that I was able to become transparent with people who were dealing with depression. I was able to talk about how He delivered me. He delivered me not only from myself but from the expectation of what the world says is a "standard."

One day I was sitting in my house and Jeremiah 31:3 (AMP) dropped into my spirit. It says, "The Lord appeared to me (Israel) from ages past, saying, "I have loved you with an everlasting love; Therefore with lovingkindness I have reminding drawn you and continued My faithfulness to you." All I could hear was the Holy Spirit telling me that its God's love for me that keeps me near Him. This scripture is the one that keeps me in a place to always know that God's love can pull you out of any situation. Depression tried to consume my life, but it was the love of God that kept my life. If you ever find yourself in a place questioning your existence or why you are here, pray and ask God to allow you to see yourself the way He sees and created you.

God did it for me when I was at the lowest point in my life, and He will do it for you. Pray this prayer as you allow God to heal you. Start your journey to healing and loving the person you see.

Father God in the Mighty Name of Jesus,

I come to you as humbly as I know how. Lord, I confess that I have allowed myself to be tormented by the enemy in my mind. I've allowed the standard of the world to take me to a place that you did not design for me. I submit my mind and thoughts over to You. Your Word says that I am fearfully and wonderfully made and the thoughts that you think towards me are good and not of evil. I stand on Your Word that I am created in Your Imagine and the likeness of You. There are no mistakes in You. I put my hand in Your hands and ask You to be my guide. Lead me through deliverance on today. I thank You. I praise You in Jesus Mighty Name I pray. Amen.

CHAPTER SIX
Disobedience

BY JOYCE HOPE

Did you know that disobedience is an attitude of the mind and finds its essence in the heart of unbelief and unfaithfulness? Disobedience according to Merriam-Webster dictionary is defined as refusal or neglect to obey rules and laws, a lack of obedience.[13] The King James Version of the Bible states in I Samuel 15:22 "...Behold to obey is better than sacrifice..." I am a witness that disobedience will cause you to forfeit the blessings that God has for you. Disobedience nearly cost me everything.

CONSEQUENCES:

Now that I've defined disobedience, I will provide 4 examples of disobedience and its consequences.

1. Moses.

He was the first person besides myself that I thought about when I decided to write on this subject. In Numbers chapter 20 verse 8 of the King James Version of the Bible, God gave Moses specific instructions "to speak ye unto the rock." In verse 11, Moses lifted his hand, and with his rod, he smote the rock twice. He was punished because of his disobedience. In Numbers chapter 20 verse 12, God spoke to Moses and said: "...therefore ye shall not bring this congregation into the land which I have given them." Because he disobeyed, Moses was not allowed to go into the Promised Land.

2. Jonah.

In the book of Jonah, He was given instructions to go down to the great city of Nineveh and cry against it. Jonah rose up, but instead of going to Nineveh, he got on a ship going in the opposite direction fleeing unto Tarshish from the presence of the Lord. By the end of the chapter, Jonah found himself in the belly of a fish for three days and three nights. Disobedience will take you on a path in life that God never intended for you to travel.

3. Nineveh.

There is another part to this story about Nineveh. In chapter 2, After Jonah's belly of the fish experience, God gave him another chance to go to Nineveh to preach unto the people. This time Jonah arose and what could have taken a 3-day journey only took Jonah one day. He preached, the people repented of their violence, turned to the Lord, and He forgave their sins. About 50 years later, in the book of Nahum, the Assyrians were back to their old ways. God sent the prophet Nahum with a message about Israel's sins. At the time Nineveh appeared invincible, but God declared He would repay them in ways that are equal to their sins.

4. Lot's wife.

Genesis 19:26 states the consequence for Lot's wife "But his wife looked back from behind him, and she became a pillar of salt." Disobedience may lead to death. Genesis 19:15-18 says "And when the morning arose, then the angels hastened Lot, saying Arise, take thy wife, and thy two daughters, which are here; lest thou be consumed in the iniquity of the city." God provided a way of escape for Lot and his family, but they lingered. They were so comfortable with the sin of Sodom and Gomorrah, that they were reluctant to leave the city. Lot even argues with the angels that are sent to rescue him on where to go for refuge. Instructions were given in verse 17 to "Escape for thy life, look not behind thee, neither stay thou in all the plain, escape to the mountain, lest thou be consumed." Lot's wife disobeyed in verse 26, and immediately she became a pillar of salt. The Message Bible states in Luke 17:32-33 "Remember what happened to Lot's wife! If you grasp and cling to life on your terms, you'll lose it, but if you let that life go, you'll get life on God's terms. Lot's wife is remembered because of her disobedience and the consequence that came with it, which for her was death.

JOYCE'S TESTIMONY:

Now that I've given you examples of persons in the bible who have suffered because of their disobedience, let me share with you how disobedience almost cost me everything.

At the age of 23 years old, I was preparing for my big day, my wedding day, I felt within that something was not right. At the time I was not mature enough to know that it was the Holy Spirit sending me a warning signal. I continued with MY PLANS. The closer it got to the wedding date, the more things seem to be going haywire. I thought this was to be expected, so I continued with MY PLANS. The wedding day finally arrived, and everything went well. The wedding night was a big disappointment. He fell asleep in the living room. The next day we took a trip to Washington, D.C. which was supposed to be our honeymoon. Instead, it was a week full of greater disappointments. The marriage was never consummated. A month after our big wedding, he decided that "He didn't want to be married." So, he moved out and went back to his momma's house. The next five years were full of ups and downs, weight loss, hair loss, and I even quit my good state job. I was emotionally, mentally and physically drained. I was so embarrassed as I became the topic of discussion among my family and friends. He moved from state to state trying to find his way but eventually moved back to his mother's house. He kept making promises that he would come back home and work on our marriage, but he never did.

I had to decide on whether to stay on this merry go round with him or to walk away. It was never his intention to be or remain married. He was one of those DL (down-low) brothers who gets married to cover up their lifestyle outside of the church. The Holy Spirit knew that, and He tried to protect me. He sent warnings, but I was naïve and spiritually immature. I did not understand the unctions of the Holy Spirit. My disobedience to the promptings of the Holy Spirit caused me to go through years of feeling rejected which only magnified my childhood feelings of abandonment from my father. I finally divorced him. A year after the divorced was finalized, I married a guy whom I met while I was separated from my husband. Big Mistake. I jumped out of the pan right into the fire. I did not give myself time to heal from the wounds that occurred during my first marriage. I was not at total peace about getting married, but again, I disobeyed the Holy Spirit. Why? Because I wanted to have sex. As a teenager in church, we were taught to wait on God to bless you with a mate, so that we would not be unequally yoked. I had waited, but he turned out to be a counterfeit aka "A Hot Potato." I had been sexually molested at the age of 7 years old, exposing me to desires of lust and perversion at an early age. In my mind, getting married was the answer to my problem, so I thought.

Now I find myself in a marriage to a man who thought his life mission was to control my life. I was trying to fill a void that only God can fill. I was looking for love in all the wrong places. My disobedience only allowed the devil to prey on those weak areas of my life. The next 22 years were full of turmoil. Since this was my second marriage, I tried my best to make it work. I was so miserable. I tolerated his immature, controlling, toxic and insecure behavior. It became abusive mentally, emotionally, financially, and sexually. He did not physically abuse me, but he often neglected the kids and me. All of this happened to me because I disobeyed the Holy Spirit.

He did not physically abuse me, but he often neglected me and the kids. He would always put everyone in front of us, especially his family whatever they wanted from him they got it because "that's my family he would say". Meanwhile, it was always an argument when asked to do something for me and the kids. He never understood the leave/cleave scripture in the bible that states, "Therefore shall a man leave his father and mother and shall cleave unto his wife, and they shall be one" (Genesis 2:24). Everyone's requests were always more important than us. I call it a public success but a private failure. This is what happened to me because I disobeyed the Holy Spirit.

I got much more than I bargained for. Today, I'm content living in an apartment with my two adult children (one disabled). I could have had a house, but the cost of it was too high. Not the price of the house but the cost of living in a toxic household. I would rather live in peace. Isaiah 32:18 says, "And my people shall dwell in a peaceable habitation and in sure dwellings and in quiet resting places."

GOD'S REDEMPTION:

But our God has a way to turn lemons into lemonade. The Bible states in Romans 8:28-30, "We know that God is always at work for the good of everyone who loves him. They are the ones God has chosen for his purpose, and he has always known who his chosen ones would be. And having chosen them, he called them to come to him. And he gave them right standing with himself, and he promised them his glory." For God is working in you, giving you the desire to obey him and the power to do what pleases him (Philippians 2:13). No matter what you have done, God can turn your mess into a message. He has done it for me. Psalms 30:11-12 says, "Thou hast turned for me my mourning into dancing: thou hast put off my sackcloth and girded me with gladness. To the end that my glory may sing praise to thee, and not be silent: O Lord my God, I will give thanks unto thee forever".

Perhaps you have found yourself in a state of disobedience. We serve a merciful God, and He waits patiently for us to come back to him. For some, it was a sermon, but for me, it was a song. My deliverance came when I heard the song "Calling My Name" by Bishop Hezekiah Walker and the Love Fellowship Choir. I listened carefully to the words repeatedly, and that song gave me hope for my future. Then one day, I stopped and repented to God for trying to do life my way. I then asked God to take control of my life. I started praying, fasting, and reading the Word of God. It wasn't a slow process, but he is a rewarder of them that diligently seek Him (Hebrews 11:6). He has done just that for me, and He will do the same for you. For there is no respect of persons with God (Romans 2:11). He loves us all the same. Francis Frangipane quotes "...When the Spirit shows you areas of sin, it is not to condemn you, but to cleanse you."

I've learned that every person I meet can teach me something. But that does not mean that person can go with me into my next level in life. I've also learned that God our Father knows what's best for me. The Bible tells us to trust in the Lord with all our heart and lean not to our own understanding. In all thy ways acknowledge Him, and he shall direct thy paths (Proverbs 3:5-6).

Father God in the name of Jesus,

I come to you with a repenting heart asking You to forgive me for all the times that I have disobeyed Your instructions and Your Word. Father, I ask You for the strength to persevere through all the negativity and tactics of the devil that I may obey You in all things. Your Word says, "Behold, to obey is better than sacrifice (1 Samuel 15:22)." Father create in me a clean heart and renew the right spirit within me. Father give me a willing and obedient spirit. I desire is to serve you with all my heart and to be obedient to You in all things. Father, You know what is best for me, and I trust You with my life. I thank You for Your grace and mercy. I receive all that You have for me from this day forward, in Jesus name. Amen.

CHAPTER SEVEN
Divorce

BY BRIDGET JEFFERSON

According to the Merriam-Webster Dictionary, divorce is to legally dissolve one's marriage with, to end by divorce, to dissolve one's marriage contract.[14] The Bible states in Malachi 2:16 (NIV), "I hate divorce says the Lord God of Israel, because the man who divorces his wife, covers his garment with violence." Even though God hated divorce, Matthew 19:9 says, "And I say unto you, Whosoever shall put away his wife, except it be for fornication, and shall marry another, committeth adultery: and whoso marrieth her which is put away doth commit adultery." Many consequences of divorce can be very costly.

CONSEQUENCES

1. Loneliness

Loneliness can be very hard to deal with especially during late nights or late in the midnight hour when there is no one to talk to or to hold you. You may find yourself entering relationships trying to fill that gap. You may even turn to social media or dating websites for some communication. Loneliness will have you looking for someone to make you smile again. It will have you desiring someone to make you feel like a woman. Be careful and realize that there are many predators out looking for that woman with low self-esteem. A predator will tell you all the things you want to hear. He may sound like the perfect man. They always do. Then you find yourself hurting again. There's a chance of being used.

2. Anger

You may begin to feel like "all men are the same." You may start to yell at your kids all the time or talk bad about their dad. Your actions may, in turn, have your children resenting their father or even you. You may feel you don't want to be in a relationship again. You may be mad at the world.

3. Fear

Fear can isolate you from the ones you love. You may not know what to do with yourself. You may be afraid to make any moves, which makes it almost impossible to move on. You may not know how to move on. Depending upon how long you were married, he may be all that you know. You will make many mistakes.

4. Financial

Depending on who the breadwinner was in your marriage, you may have to downsize by moving from a house to an apartment.

You may have to get a job. Maybe you've never worked before, and you may have to get a second job. You might not get child support. It won't be easy.

5. Guilt

You may ask yourself, "What have I done? Maybe I should have stayed with him? What could I have done differently?" You may think, "I can't do this. There must be a better way." The children may blame you. You may blame yourself.

BRIDGET'S TESTIMONY

I was with my now ex-husband for twenty years. I was twenty years old, and he was twenty-six years old. I had an eighteen-month-old daughter from a previous relationship. He had just been released from prison after being locked up for ten years. He was still legally married to another woman. Since he was living with his mother and not his wife, I thought he was fair game. I was so young and naive. He was such a handsome man and resembled Denzel Washington to me. I remember the first time he told me he loved me. I had never been told that before, so I just looked at him in amazement. I couldn't say a word. He then told me, "It's okay, you don't have to love me right now, but you will." He had a way with words, and I began to fall in love with him. I never imagined myself without him.

As I reflect, I remember people saying to me, "How did you end up with him?" He was a street man, and I was shy and quiet. But you know what they say, "Good girls always want the bad boys." He soon became a drug dealer in the street. I didn't like it, but I had fallen in love with this man. I remember the first time I became pregnant. I was having twins. We were so happy and excited. But I ended up losing the babies. I had what they called a blighted ovum. Blighted Ovum is where the babies disintegrate, and I ended up having a miscarriage. I quickly became pregnant again. By the time I was five months pregnant, our apartment was raided for drugs. The police threatened to arrest me. My ex-husband told them I was pregnant and that I had nothing to do with the drugs.

When I heard him tell the police that, I fell more in love because I thought he must love me. I felt I had to be there for him. I gave birth four months later to our oldest son. My ex-husband was released from prison two years later. He came home, and I became pregnant again. He was selling drugs. We moved into a beautiful house in a better neighborhood. I never like the fact that he was a drug dealer, I just dealt with it. About a year after I gave birth to our second son, he was arrested again. This time, he was sentenced to ten years. I was strong, faithful and true to him. We married in jail. When we married, I somehow knew in my spirit, we should not marry. But I didn't listen. The number one reason I married him was to prove to others that he would marry me. The second reason was that we had children. The third reason was that I loved him.

Every three months like clockwork, we had family reunion visits (conjugal visits) which is another world. Many women marry men they don't even know. I became pregnant with our 3rd son. Though we were together in the streets and already started a family, many women have children for men who are sentenced to life. There are many reasons such as loneliness and low self-esteem. Also, some women feel they have control in the marriage. These visits are set up like a regular home. There was a two-bedroom apartment with a full kitchen, a playground for the kids, barbeque grill, bicycles, and basketball court. I'd cook full course meals. It was very comfortable, but all behind the gates of a prison. I had a fulltime job at a local hospital. I still had to pay the bills. I still had to maintain a life outside which was exhausting. I did those ten years with him faithfully. I was there for him. I didn't even look at another man.

In my mind, because I reaped the benefits of him selling drugs, I was supposed to be there for him. Even though he cheated so many times, I still felt he loved me. He was always good to me. But he had a way of making me feel like, no one else would want me, without saying those words. I thought he could have any woman he wanted. He was released and came home after serving the full ten years. Mentally, I was in another place. I had a good job and a new car that I had purchased myself. There's nothing like being able to take care of yourself, financially. I just wanted him to do right, get a job and be a family. But he came home and began to cheat. We had three teenagers, and they saw what was going on. They saw him with another woman, and it did not sit well with them. One of the women became pregnant which was the last straw for me. My mother had found out. She came to me, and said, "I will have your back in whatever you decide to do. If you choose to stay with him, I got your back. If you choose to leave, I got your back." She understood either way. As my mother, she wanted me to leave. She just wanted me to have the strength.

Through all that I was going through, I began to have a reoccurring dream of my mom. In this dream, I would see her lying in my bed. There was a bright light at the head of my bed. She'd reach her hand out as she called out to my grandmother who had passed away some years ago. I had this dream for about a month. My mom was to have surgery on her rotator cuff. I told my mom about this dream. She was sold out saved, sanctified, and full of the Holy Ghost. She looked at me and paused. She said, "Well, we will just pray about that." There was a weird look on her face. The surgery went well. But on the day she was to be released from the hospital, I got a call from her doctor. He said they had found her lying on the floor in the bathroom. They resuscitated her about five times. She died on Mother's Day 2006. Her death was the hardest thing I ever had to deal with. I fell into a deep depression. My mom was gone. I had no one. Both sets of my grandparents had died in the midst of the years my husband was in jail. At this point, I no longer wanted to be married. I know my mom prayed for me. She always told me that God was dealing with me. I didn't understand what she meant.

I began to pray like never before. I learned to pray unselfishly. I remember coming home from work on a Friday night. God was starting to speak to me. I remember hearing God talk to me. He said, "If you ever want to be happy, it won't be with him." I was like wow! I couldn't believe I just heard that. I dropped to my knees and cried out to God. I said, "God, I feel like I don't want to be married anymore. If this is the man that you have for me, then tell me what I need to do. If there is someone else out there that you have just for me, then let him go." God is amazing, three days later, on Monday, I was at work when I got a phone call that my husband had been arrested. I knew that was God. I didn't have the strength to leave, and he wouldn't. He went to jail for yet another year. That year quickly went by. He was calling me. He said, "Parole will be calling you so I can come home." I said, "Okay."

God is so amazing. Parole began to call me. The phone rang and rang. I reached my hand out to pick up the phone, and I froze. I could not touch the phone. His brother called, I could not answer the phone. That was a supernatural move of God. He did not allow me to answer that phone. It was not me. There was no other explanation. God was at work. I praise Him for that because I did not have the strength. So my ex-husband was released. With nowhere to go, he went to live with the woman he's now married to, not the one that had the baby for him. He was no longer my problem. He was very upset with me. We didn't speak for a year, and then he started coming back around. We began to have a sexual relationship. I didn't care that he was living with another. We were still married, and I had needs. That was short lived. I began to feel like, "I don't want to do this anymore. I'm doing to her. What did she do to me?" I didn't feel right, so I left him alone. God had spoken to me again. He said, "He seems happy, but in the end, she will see him for who he really is." That wasn't my problem.

I was still very depressed after the death of my mom. It had taken a toll on me. I had gained a lot of weight. I was in so much physical pain. I had high blood pressure, nerve pain, and my bloodwork showed evidence of a type of blood cancer. But GOD. I had many cardiac workups, headaches, and I even had brain surgery. After having a brain MRI, it showed that I had a condition called Chiari Malformation. It is a condition where part of your brain grows into your spine. It causes headaches and dizziness. In 2009, I had decompression surgery. The surgeons took a piece of bone out of the back of my head to relieve pressure off my brain. This was small for me, but many are disabled and confined to a wheelchair. I am blessed. I would have never had this surgery if I wasn't depressed. I didn't care if I lived or died at that time. But God. As I healed from the surgery, my middle son began to have seizures. This was very scary. I had never seen anything like this. One morning as I slept, my son who was seventeen at the time, woke me up. He said mom, "My chest hurts when I cough."

So, I got up and began to get dressed. My son went into a seizure. Blood was coming from his mouth. I called the paramedics, and we went to the hospital. They did x-rays and said one of his lungs collapsed. So, I sat with him waiting to go to a room. When he began to have another seizure, he had coded. When I saw him again, the doctors said that the other lung was going. They put my son in an induced coma. My son went to the ICU and was on a ventilator which is a machine that was breathing for him. As I stood there looking at my baby, I said to myself, "OMG! I'm about to bury my son."

I heard the voice of God again. He said, "No you're not. He is not going anywhere." I just began to cry. I slept on a cot behind him in the ICU. I could not leave. I prayed and prayed. I heard the doctor come in the next morning. The nurse said to him, "Do you think he will make it?" The doctor quickly replied," I have faith." About 30 minutes later, the doctor came to get me. He said, "Come. I want you to see something." I ran behind the doctor. He began to show me x-rays of my son's lungs. They were coming back. Praise God! My son is now twenty-six years old. I know God has something in store for him. I was still very depressed, but God spoke to me again. He said, " Your kids need you." God began to pull me out of depression. Amen. It was time for me to stand up again. It was a struggle, but God brought me through the storm. When God is trying to get your attention, and you don't listen, you will go through.

Isaiah 55:8-9 (NIV) says, "For my thoughts are not your thoughts, neither are your ways my ways" declares the Lord. As the heavens are higher than the earth, so are my ways higher than your ways, and my thoughts than your thoughts."

GOD'S REDEMPTION

I began to date. I met so many of the wrong men. Either they were already in a relationship, or they were trying to move in. I even met men that turned out to be bisexual and wanted me to have a woman. Another was fifty years old and wanted to be a rapper. At this point, I said to myself, "This must be a joke." I began to pray harder and harder. I said, "Lord, clearly I can't pick them." I dropped to my knees, I said, "Lord, I want what you have for me. I don't care what he looks like, what he got, or ain't got. If you have him for me, I can't go wrong. All I asked is that he be a man that would bring me closer to you, God." Every time I met a man, I would say, "Lord, is that him?" I never heard a word. I just stayed in prayer.

Then one day while on Facebook, I got an inbox from a guy that I remembered from back in my high school days. I was like, "Here we go again." So many men are always talking trash in the inbox. So, I hadn't seen this guy in thirty years. We began to text and talk. We were texting for about six hours straight. I would not let him call me. As we were texting, I heard the voice of God. He said, "That is your husband." I was amazed. I began to look through his page more. I was like, "OMG! He's a pastor. I don't know about that Lord., I hadn't been to church in years." But I asked God for a man that would bring me closer to Him. We were married thirty days later.

As I moved to Atlanta, God began to work in me quickly. I surrendered to God. My gifts began to grow. I have been a dreamer all my life since the age of eight. I started to have visions within three months. As I continued to grow and experienced many things, I am now 1st lady and Elder Bridget Jefferson. My husband is Overseer Bryndon Jefferson, Pastor, and founder of Forever Faithful Christian Ministries here in Atlanta Georgia. I bless God for all that I have been through and all that I'm going through. For it has made me the woman I am today. There is more that I'm going through that is making me the woman I am to be. We must have faith and trust in God. For He can and will bring you through the impossible.

Hebrews 11:1 says, "Now faith is the substance of things hoped for, the evidence of things not seen."

Lord, I come to you humbled. Lord, I love you. Lord, I adore you. I thank You for saving me. I thank You for making me the woman that I am today. Lord, I would go through it all over again to have what I have in you. Lord, I ask that you continue to have Your way in my life. I ask that You send a whirlwind of warring and Healing Angels my way. Lord, saturate every bone, vessel, vein, and nerve in my body to be filled and flooded with the precious Blood of Jesus. The Blood of Jesus! Have Your way, Lord. Have Your way in Jesus Mighty Name. Have Your way. Amen.

CHAPTER EIGHT
Domestic Violence

BY JOY MARTIN

Have you thought about domestic violence being a worldwide epidemic? Before I take you into my devastation, allow me to provide you with definitions and statics that you may find quite disturbing. It may give you a different perspective on domestic violence. First, Merriam-Webster defines domestic violence as the inflicting of physical injury by one family or household member on another.[15]

Proverbs 6:16-19 says, "These six things the LORD hates, Yes, seven are an abomination to Him: A proud look, A lying tongue, Hands that shed innocent blood, A heart that devises wicked plans, Feet that are swift in running to evil, A false witness who speaks lies, And one who sows discord among brethren."

Secondly, domestic violence can be so detrimental on so many ways levels. According to the National Coalition Against Domestic Violence, on average nearly twenty people per minute are physically abused by an intimate partner in the United States. For one year, this equates to more than 10 million women and men.[16] Did you hear about the most startling static to date by the United Nations? The home is the most dangerous place for women. According to their study, more than half the women who were murdered worldwide in 2017 were killed by the partner or by family members.[17] I can personally say, that I was a part of the static count over twenty years ago. However, that static did not define my destiny.

CONSEQUENCES

Even though I was not in an ongoing abusive relationship –this was a onetime occurrence. However, there are still consequences that followed this life-altering event.

1. Fear

I lived in fear for quite some time after the ordeal. Dealing with the aftermath of this event took its toll on me after a while. I kept changing my schedule, always held the restraining order on me, and always looked over my shoulders. I finally understood that fear was a spirit that attempted to paralyze me for good. Praise God, fear was finally eradicated from my life. 2 Timothy 1:7 states, "For God has not given us a spirit of fear, but of power and of love and of a sound mind." I gained my life back and my power back.

2. Shame

Shame was one of the emotional consequences that I endured after the event. Because I had never been in a situation like that before, nor ever imagined that I could be involved in a traumatic event like that. Shame stalked me for many years until I surrendered and relinquished my old self by leaving it at the cross. I made an exchange with shame for double honor at the foot of the Cross.

Isaiah 61:7 states, "Instead of your shame you shall have double honor, and instead of confusion they shall rejoice in their portion. Therefore, in their land they shall possess double; Everlasting joy shall be theirs."

3. Bitterness

Out of all my consequences, bitterness was the most dangerous consequences that overtook me and consumed me. The Bible clearly warns us in Ephesians 4:31 (NKJV), "Let all bitterness, wrath, anger, [a]clamor, and evil speaking be put away from you, with all malice." Now that we have covered some of the consequences connected to Domestic Violence, journey with me as I share my personal story of how it cost me everything!

JOY'S TESTIMONY

I once heard the expression, "it takes one second for your whole life to change." Well, I found out that saying was true. Over twenty years ago, in one second, my life drastically changed forever. I was a young mother at that time. My son's father, Larry and I, were no longer together as a couple. We had agreed that it was better for us to stay apart and co-parent our son. We had successfully moved on in our personal lives, both of us were in new relationships. My son's grandmother was his regular babysitter. However, Friday's our schedule changed slightly. I would drop my son off at his grandmother's house on Friday mornings then head off to work. But when I got off from work, I would go to Larry's house to pick up our son. This was our regular routine every Friday. When I went to pick up my son after work, Larry was acting so bizarre. I didn't understand what was going on. Larry's new girlfriend was there, but that didn't bother me. I could not figure out why he was acting so strange. Larry always had a very calm and quiet demeanor, so I was thrown off by his behavior.

All the years that we had been together, I had never seen Larry act like this before. Larry kept saying, "Why are you here"? I repeatedly stated, "I am here to pick up Trey. "This is the routine, what are you talking about?" We do this every Friday." I will never forget the look in his eyes. Since I did not grow up in the church, I had no concept of the spiritual realm. I had no understanding of the Kingdom of God nor the Kingdom of Satan. I had never heard of demons or demonic oppression. I am now fully aware that the enemy had a complete plan to destroy me. I will always remember the look in Larry's eyes. Larry, the one that I had known for years, was not the person that was staring back at me. It was demons on assignment trying to take me out!

Larry was screaming at me from the top of his lungs. He was so close to my face. He could have bit my lip off. I was so confused. I did not understand what was happening. Larry was screaming, "You're not taking Trey home!" "He's not going anywhere!" "He's staying with me, and I will bring him to you when I want you to have him!" It was as if time stopped. Everything happened so fast. Before I knew it, Larry had thrown me to the floor, sat on my stomach and began to punch me in my face like I was a natural grown man. His girlfriend was screaming and trying to pull him off me. Then I saw Trey, out of the corner of my eye. He was jumping up and down and screaming Mommy! Mommy! I told the girlfriend to get Trey out of there. Larry then dragged me down the steps by my hair and threw me out the door as if I was yesterday's garbage.

When I came to myself, the neighbors were all outside, just staring at me. Cell phones were not the norm back then. I ran around the corner to the pay phone to call the police. I had no quarters in my pockets, just bills. Some of the neighbors followed me around the corner. I started hysterically throwing bills at people, begging them for quarters. I heard someone say go home and call the police as one lady tried to put my money back in my pockets. I was in total shock. I didn't know where the girlfriend had taken my son. I could barely see because while he was punching me in my face, he shattered my glasses. I'm screaming at the operator, about what happened and that I didn't know where my baby was. She told me the police would help me find my baby but don't return to the scene. She kept asking me where I was. My mind went blank. I couldn't tell her where I was. Some of the people that were standing around me told her my location. I hung up and called my father, left a message on his answer machine. I called my mom at work, left another message. It felt like forever, before the police showed up. They tried to calm me down so I could explain everything that happened. Then it felt like the crowd moved in unison. The officers, neighbors and I walked back around the corner.

I saw the girlfriend sitting on the steps. She had rocked Trey to sleep. The police entered the house looking for Larry, but he wasn't there. They asked me did I want to go to the hospital. I declined. I just wanted to go to my father's house. My father lived about 20 minutes away from Larry. I pleaded with the police to take me to my father's house. I was in no condition to be walking. I could barely see anything because of my broken glasses. The police told me they could not put me in their squad car because I did not commit a crime. I had to walk all those blocks in mental, emotional, and physical anguish. I was completely discombobulated, vision distorted and still bleeding. The man that I once loved and now my abuser, appeared out of nowhere! He started following me and saying, "I can't believe you called the police, I'm going to kill you!" "I'm going to take you out!" Now, here I am running down the street pushing a stroller crying even more.

I grew up in the inner city of Baltimore. In the hood, our area was densely populated with drugs. The drug dealers "owned" the corners and the sidewalk. So, when you wanted to walk down the street, you could not use the sidewalk. You literally had to step out into the street. To this day, I had never seen anything like it. All the thugs and drug dealers that never moved, all moved out of my way that night. It was if the Red Sea had parted and complete silence took over as they backed out of our way.

A man stepped out from the crowd who looked like a drug addict. He had the smell of alcohol oozing out of his pores. I had not seen him before. He was dressed differently from the drug dealers, not too neat. He started walking with me asking, "What's wrong?" "What happened?" I was too traumatized to talk. All I could do at that time was push Trey's stroller. I just wanted to get to my father's house. This man kept asking me questions trying to make sure I was okay. He wanted to know if I was bleeding anywhere else. He showed such great concern for my wellbeing, but I was too overwhelmed to answer him. He then said," Sister, I'm going to walk with you. Ain't nobody else gonna touch you." It was like I was in a trance. I heard everything the man had said, but I couldn't respond. It seemed like I walked forever to get to my father's house. Then I finally turned the corner. I saw my father and my mother standing on the steps looking from both ends of the block trying to see the direction I'd be coming. When I saw my parents, I started running towards them.

I saw my father as he started walking down the steps. He was making his way down the street towards us. He stopped abruptly, turned around and started running back to the house. Then a few minutes later, my father came down those steps on a mission to kill whoever was responsible for hurting his baby girl. I know that my mother was no physical match for my father, but by the grace of Almighty God, she was able to get my father and his gun back up those steps and into the house. When I reached my mother, I collapsed in her arms. My mother told me later that the man who walked with me picked up Trey's stroller and took him upstairs into the house. Years later, the Holy Spirit said to me that the man was an angel and was sent to walk along with me. I had no idea at that time that I was entertaining an angel unaware.

I finally worked up the nerve to look in the mirror that evening. I could not believe my eyes. I flipped out all over again. My face swollen, lip busted, and my hair ripped out of my scalp. I was bruised all over my body from the punching and being dragged down a flight of stairs. My family tried to convince me to go to the hospital, but I refused. Shame, embarrassment, and disbelief settled in. The more they insisted that I go to the hospital, the more I resisted. As the night came, my family and I were still in disbelief. My son slept through most of it. My sister took care of the Trey the rest of the night. I didn't want him to see me like that.

My man or my boyfriend, Tony, and I had plans that night. It was well after the time that we were supposed to hook up. My mom called him for me and did most of the talking. I asked him to come over my dad's house, but Tony refused. It was the first time that Tony had no words to say. He couldn't believe it. After a long pause, He just kept saying, "He did what?" I wanted him to come over for comfort and support. Tony said, "I don't think it's a good idea for me to see you like that. I may do something that I will regret." Tony said, "I will call to check on you several times a day, but I can't handle seeing you like that." He asked me to let him know when all the physical evidence had disappeared and that he would see me then.

I didn't go back to my apartment at all that week. I stayed at my father's house. The next morning, my mother or sister called Larry's mother. She knew something was wrong because no one in my family had ever called her before. She became frantic, "What's going on?" she said. "Joy is here every morning at six, and she didn't call. That's not like her". They told her what happened. She became irate and said, "He would never do anything like that." My son would never touch her. He would never hit a woman; not Joy he loves her." She said, "He called this morning and wanted to know if she was here and when I told him no, he just hung up." She was in unbelief that her son could do something this horrific. This event profoundly impacted everyone.

I never went to the hospital, but I went to the police station to file an ex parte order (restraining order). They explained to me to make as many copies as I needed; that I must always keep the ex parte order with me and on my person. In Baltimore City, there are Domestic Violence court hearings every Monday. Just let that sink in for a moment. Every Monday, there was a courtroom solely designated just for this epidemic; and this was over twenty years ago. So here I am in a courtroom full of woman that had experienced the same thing that I did. I was appointed a Lawyer from the House of Ruth. My life had drastically changed, every Monday I was in court waiting for him to show up. A bench warrant was put out for his arrest. For fifty-two Mondays, my life was on hold. All the physical evidence, of course, had disappeared by then, but emotionally I was falling apart. I was mentally exhausted. It was one of the longest years of my life.

During that year, many things had transpired. Tony and I became even closer than before. He was there for me during one of the darkest periods of my life. Tony promised me that he'd never raise a hand to me, disrespect me, or hurt me like that. He said because of everything that has happened that he didn't want to keep any secrets from me anymore. Fear gripped me because I didn't know what Tony was going to say. He wanted me to promise that I wouldn't leave him after he poured out and barred all. My first thought was that maybe he was married. But the bomb that he dropped on me, I was not at all prepared for and could have never guessed it. He told me that he was a professional hit man. I screamed at him, "You're a what!" "You kill people for a living?" "You must be kidding me!" "Tony this is not funny!" "Is this some twisted joke?" I was shocked. He kept saying, "Just let me explain." I thought to myself that there was nothing to explain. "I am ready to walk away from that lifestyle for us," he said. I was in love with a hit man. I stayed with him. It was a secret that we shared that I could not utter to anyone else. We never talked about it again.

I went to church for the first time since I was a little girl during that year as well. I gave my life to Jesus Christ during that service. I honestly did open my mouth and believed in my heart and asked Jesus Christ into my heart and my life. I was serious and meant every word that I said, but I still had the streets deeply embedded in me. After, a long, exhausting year, Larry finally appeared in court. The judge stated, "Since you have never been in trouble before, you have a clean record, I believe that you had a lapse in judgment that day. Therefore, I'm going to sentence you to eighteen months of anger-management classes, three years of probation, and you must pay restitution for her glasses because when you punched her in her face, you broke her glasses." He was considered a good guy in the hood.

I fell apart at his sentencing. I could not believe this was happening. I was expecting him to serve time in jail! All I could think was because he didn't have a long rap sheet, he gets a slap on the wrist for being naughty? I was traumatized all over again! Thinking of the past year and all that Trey and I endured. Our lives were re-arranged for the entire year. I traveled in fear many times wondering if he was going to show up. I always kept all my ex parte orders on me, just in case Larry assaulted me again. Because of the trauma, Trey needed counseling. Because he saw everything that transpired, he could not sleep. When he did fall asleep, he would be fighting in sleep, calling for me. Trey had begun to regress from this horrific event. I worked very hard with Trey to wean him from the bottle, pacifier, and potty-training him. Just like that, trauma came and stole it. It was like it never happened. We had both been traumatized so much that previous year and now this!

Anger and bitterness came in, sat down on my broken heart and refused to budge. I thought to myself, "He's getting away with a slap on the wrist. Trey and I suffer because he had a clean record and never broke the law before." I snapped! I decided to take him out! I said, "There's no justice in the justice system!" I'm going to kill him!" There is no way that he can keep living on this green earth and act as if nothing happened. He must pay for what he did to Trey and me. I had officially gone over the cliff. There was no return.

Tony came over that night, and I told him what happened in court that day. Tony couldn't believe that's all he got too. Tony was trying to console me, but I was enraged. I told Tony that I was going to kill Larry. He said, "You're going to do what?" "You're just upset." "You don't have a mean bone in your body." "You can't kill a fly." "Just calm down, and we will get through this too." But I wasn't trying to hear all of that. I wanted to make Larry suffer for what he did to me. I finally admitted that I couldn't kill anyone. I am going to hire someone to take him out! Tony continued to try to calm me down. He said I was not thinking clearly, and that I should lay down, etc. I was not going to let him get away with what he did to me, so he was going to have to die. Then I told Tony because I was a single mama and I didn't have a whole lot of money that I needed him to do it for me. I told him, "I need you to take him out because he does not deserve to live!" Tony said, "You just you need just to calm down because you don't mean it."

As the conversion continued, Tony was making me angrier. He was not taking me seriously. "The police told you that they would take care of everything and it's good to press changes etc." I went through all of that for this, NO!! He must suffer for what he did to me. I will get my justice because the justice system let me down. I told Tony, "Since you are a professional hit man, it will be very easy for you to do this." Tony begins to explain to me, "When you cross that bridge, you cannot return from it. That's not something you want to get involved in... it's a dark side that comes with all of that. You are one of the kindest persons that I know. You don't want to travel down that road. I am leaving that life behind for us. I used to be a hit man, but I am NOT going to kill him for you."

I started acting crazy, and I went ballistic on him. I began hurling insults at him like, "I thought you loved me. I thought that you would do anything for me. You lied to me. You don't love me at all." I said, "You do this for a living so why wouldn't you do it for me? People hire you to kill. This is crazy. Now the killer got morals and ethical codes. You said you would do anything for me. I thought you loved Trey like your own child. You don't love me if you are not willing to kill for me. Get out of my house!!" I kicked Tony out of my house. I became someone that I didn't even recognize. I became a manipulative bully!

Every time Tony called, I wouldn't answer, or I would hang up on him. This went on for weeks. Then Tony called one day and said, "I am coming over. I need to talk to you, and you better let me in." Tony handed me a stack of mail. And I asked, "What's this?" He kept saying look at it. It was all of Larry's mail. I said, "Did you take care of him?" Tony said, "No, I just wanted you to see how close I was to him. I could have done if I wanted to. Joy, I do love you. I do love Trey like he is my son. But this is not how you do things. I was a professional hit man. It's just simply business. They paid me, and I killed. This is emotional. I can't kill him. I love you enough to say no. Do you think I can come over here and look in Trey's face knowing I killed his father?" I said, "Oh, so now you got a heart? I wasn't hearing it.

I took that mail and threw it at him. I told him, "I don't need no post man, I need a killer." I kicked him out again!

Bitterness, hatred, and rage turned me into someone that I could no longer identify. None of my friends or family knew what was going on all this time. I was a professional actress. Smiling and wearing a mask all along but falling to pieces on the inside. The only one that I had confided in about all of this was Tony. Now months had gone by, and Tony was still leaving me messages. I kept telling him it was over between us. I became obsessed with trying to find a way to make Larry suffer. I didn't have enough money to hire a professional hit man like Tony, so my next best thing was to get a functional junkie.

A functional junkie is a professional business person who had an addiction to drugs. They were not the average drug user that I would see strung out on the corner or the ones that steal everything to pawn it to get high again. These professionals worked regular jobs, yet they knew exactly what time to stop getting high. They knew how long it would take before that high would wear off and prepare themselves to go back to work in the morning. When they get off from work or get out of school, they hit it. They hit it hard. They hit it quick, and they come off.

I started plotting and planning how to kill Larry. I got a composition book and began to write out my plan. I used to deliver newspapers with him early in the morning like 3 am. I knew his route. I also know that if I didn't go with him, then his brother would go with him. He never delivered papers alone. I came up with a plan. To make it look like a robbery, I would have his brother shot in the leg or arm, but Larry killed. I had the whole plan written in my book. Sometimes I would tell myself that I was crazy, but it wasn't enough to stop me from what I was doing. I was in the mirror practicing my facial expressions and what I would say when Larry's mother would call me and give me the news that her son was dead. Two years have gone by since that devastating Friday evening. I knew no one would put the pieces together and think that it was me. But I was still engulfed with bitterness. The only thing that gave me solace was that he was going to die soon.

I was still going to church during this entire time. I was a faithful member of that church where I gave my life to Jesus Christ. I was going to Worship services on Sundays & Bible Study every Wednesday night. But I had never had a real encounter with the Living God! So, when people tell me "I go to church," that doesn't mean anything to me. I know firsthand that killers go to church too. I went to church twice a week, singing in the choir and serving in the community while the entire time my mind was consumed with revenge. The Word was being preached and taught, but it never really penetrated my heart. Yes, I was a church goer, but my soul needed deliverance. My mind was polluted, and my heart was full of wickedness.

GOD'S REDEMPTION

I had decided that I was ready to move to the next phase of my plan. I had to memorize everything that was in my book because I was prepared to burn it and to start making payments to my functional junkie. I was up most of the night, just walking back and forth in my living room and reading my plans out loud while trying to get all the details embedded inside of me. Suddenly, during my rehearsal, I hear a voice say, "Don't do it!" I went back to my bedroom, and Trey was sound asleep. I went to the windows, lifted the blinds, and no one was there. I went to the front door, and no one was there. The television and the radio were not on. But that voice was crystal clear. It startled me because I know what I heard. No one was there. After some time had passed, I began to laugh it off. I thought, "Wow! I am officially crazy because now I hear voices."

After I waited for a little while longer, I picked my book back up and went back to rehearsing my plan again. I heard the same audible voice again. It was as if someone was standing right beside me. But this time the voice was louder and much firmer. DON'T DO IT! I heard it in my ear, yet simultaneously I felt it in my spirit. I immediately went crashing to the floor.

It was like a Damascus Road experience. I knew it was the Lord. I had been sitting in church for over a year, yet never had an encounter with Him. After I hit the floor, I began to cry uncontrollably. I cried out for Jesus to save me! Instantly, I was in my right frame of mind to make an intelligent decision. I repented unto the Lord. I had asked him to forgive me for all the things that I had done. I had godly sorrow in my heart. I asked the Lord to heal my broken heart. True conversion took place that night. Because God intervened that night, Larry did not die. I did not end up in jail and Trey did not end up losing both of his parents. Over time, I eventually told Larry the whole story. He was in unbelief, yet grateful that I never followed through with my plan. Now, Trey is a grown man. Larry and I get along very well. After my heart was totally restored, I knew that I had to reconnect with Tony. I shared the entire encounter with him, and I asked for his forgiveness. He forgave me. He also saw that I was a different person. In time, he gave his heart to Jesus Christ. Tony and I are still good friends to this very day.

I want you to know, that I cultivated a personal relationship with Jesus Christ for real. I was going to church and praying out of formality, yet I had never experienced the power of God. Up till that point, I never knew that you could hear the voice of the Lord. The Lord met me that night in my living room. I will always remember that. God stepped in, intervened, and saved my life. He rescued me from the grips of the enemy. I began to read my bible and pray to my Abba Father daily. I was confident that He heard my prayers. I fell in love with the Lord. Oh, He is the lover of my soul. I eventually discovered that the enemy knew more about my destiny than I did. That is why he was trying to destroy me. I ultimately found out that I had a call on my life to serve King Jesus and His people. Over time, the call was confirmed again and again. I matured in the things of the Lord. I am grateful that I can now say, that I have been serving in His Kingdom for many years now. I have no regrets. I am the woman that I am today because of this encounter and countless others with the Lord. I am truly honored that I Get to Serve the King!!

Abuse of any kind is so damaging on so many levels. No matter how small or insignificant you make it seem, abuse is still abuse. Abuse from anyone is wrong, and it should not occur. I challenge you to look at a familiar Bible story from a different perspective. The story of Saul and David is a very well-known Bible story. However, King Saul was an abusive authority figure towards David. Saul tried to kill David on more than one occasion. But David always fled. If you are in an abusive situation or relationship, I encourage you to get out quickly and safely.

If you are the Abuser, there is help available for you if you desire it. It is not too late for you. There are caring and supportive people available at The National Domestic Violence Hotline: 1.800.799.7233 or www.thehotline.org

PRAYER FOR THE ABUSER:

Dear Heavenly Father,

I come before you as humbly as I know how. I confess that I am sorry for my actions and my words to control, manipulate, and abuse _____. I am truly sorry and repent for my sins of being angry, violent, and hurting others. Holy Spirit help me to trust You to guide me. I yield my mind, heart, and words to you today Jesus Christ. Wash me in your blood and deliver me now. I now renounce the Spirit of anger, control, and violence from my life. I come out of agreement with you. You no longer have a stronghold on me. I now receive God's peace, gentleness, and self-control in my life. Thank you, Jesus! Amen.

If you are the one being abused, there is help available. There are caring and supportive people available that will help create an escape plan if you need one. Get the Help you need. Don't delay, call today. The National Domestic Violence Hotline: 1.800.799.7233 or www.thehotline.org

PRAYER FOR THE ONE BEING ABUSED:

Dear Heavenly Father,

I praise your mighty name. I am grateful that I am alive, and I can make a sound decision. Holy Spirit, I choose to forgive _____ for _____. I release them now. I forgive them. I bless them. God your Word says, "That you will heal the broken hearted and those that are crushed in spirit." Thank you for healing my broken heart. I surrender my mind, soul, and my body to you. Jesus, wash me in your precious blood and deliver me now. I renounce the spirit of fear, shame, unworthiness, victimization, violence, trauma, mind control, and financial bondage. I come out of agreement with you today. You demonic spirits will longer try to rule my life. Thank you, Lord, for creating me in Your beautiful image. I now receive the full measure of God's love, joy, and peace. Holy Spirit, thank You for giving me courage, wisdom, strength, and clarity for my next steps. Abba Father, thank You for Your endless protection. Thank you, Jesus, for answering my prayer! In Jesus' name. Amen.

CHAPTER NINE
Envy

BY KIMBERLY MOSES

Have you ever envied someone so much that the sight of that person made you hate them even more? Have you ever hated when someone else got blessed? If your answer is yes, then take heed. Nothing good comes out of envy. According to Merriam-Webster, envy is painful or resentful awareness of an advantage enjoyed by another joined with a desire to possess the same advantage.[18] Envying someone is an evil thing to do. Your heart will become full of wickedness. To James 3:16 says, "For where envying and strife is, there is confusion and every evil work." Envy will cost you everything. Now that we know what envy is let's discuss some of its consequences.

CONSEQUENCES

1. Sickness

Having envy in your heart can make you sick. Sickness is of the devil because it is evil. Contrarily, good things come from

God. Proverbs 14:30 says, "A sound heart is the life of the flesh: but envy the rottenness of the bones." James 1:17 says, "Every good gift and every perfect gift is from above, and cometh down from the Father of lights, with whom is no variableness, neither shadow of turning." God wants you healed and blessed. He doesn't want you to suffer from sickness when Jesus already paid the price for our healing. Isaiah 53:5 says, "But he was wounded for our transgressions, he was bruised for our iniquities: the chastisement of our peace was upon him; and with his stripes we are healed."

2. Murder

Being envious can cause you to commit murder. The devil can enter a person's heart and overwhelming them with the spirit of murder. As a result, they will end up killing the person who they don't want them to advance. It's like crabs in a pot of boiling water. When one crab reaches up to the top to escape, another crab below in the bottom of the pot pulls him back down. Cain and Abel are an excellent example of being envious. They were brothers in the book of Genesis. Cain was envious of Abel because God accepted his brother's offering instead of his. He hated his brother and killed him over it. Nothing good comes out of being envious of someone.

3. Rivalry

Being envious can result in you competing with them. It takes a lot of time and energy to compete with someone. It will rob you of peace and joy when you see the person advancing.

You will end up miserable. You won't be able to sleep or eat because you are thinking of ways to outdo them. The bible warns us about rivalry. Philippians 2:3 (ESV) says, "Do nothing from rivalry or conceit, but in humility count others more significant than yourselves." Now that we have discussed the consequences let's look at Joann's story of how envy can cost you everything!

JOANN'S STORY

Joann was an elderly widow trying to overcome loneliness. To encourage herself, she would listen to music. She loved music about love with an upbeat tempo. She started listening to this famous Asian singer name Julia Chun. She was young and beautiful. Joann became obsessed with her. She would think about her day and night. She saw a lot of herself in Julia. Joann could also sing, but her music never went anyway. Joann had to get close to Julia at all cost. Every concert Julia did, Joann was there. She studied the staff and did her research so she could find out the perfect way to enter Julia's life. One day that opportunity happened. A position opened to be on the media team. Joann knew this was her chance.

She was interviewed by a senior staff member on Julia's team. Joann's expertise about media blew the interviewer away. The interviewer was very impressed and offered Joann the job a week later. Joann was excited because she could finally get closed to Julia which wasn't as easy as she hoped it would be. Joann studied Julia's every moved. She knew what kind of food she enjoyed and her favorite spots to relax. Joann began to buy her favorite sweets and gifts along with cards. She wanted to be her friend, but Julia never returned the kindness. She wasn't returning the gratitude that Joann desired. Julia wasn't interested in being friends with any of her staff. She just wanted to finish up her tour and work on upcoming projects.

Joann felt rejected and overtime, she started to get envious of Julia. She hated how people praised her for her music and how beautiful she was. No matter how hard Joann tried to shake these negative feelings, she couldn't overcome them. She wished that people would praise her the way they praised Julia. One summer day, Joann had the opportunity to speak with Julia while she was alone in the dressing room. Joann went into her dressing room awkwardly and made up an excuse. She asked her a question about the sound in the stadium. Julia answered and went back to reading sheets of music. When she looked up, Joann was still standing in her dressing room. Julia politely asked, "Is there anything else that you need?"

Joann went off. She locked the door and started saying things such as, "You think you are so high and mighty. You look down on people like me. You don't deserve to be where you are. I should be out there singing in the auditorium. You never appreciated anything nice that I did for you." Julia was scared and didn't understand what caused Joann to react like this. She said, "Excuse me. You are crazy. You are fired. Now get out of my dressing room!" She reached for her phone to call for help, but in a moment of panic Joann picked up a guitar and smashed it over Julia's head. Julia immediately went unconscious.

Joann panicked even more. "Oh no," she thought to herself. "What have I done?" She went over to where Julia was laying, but she realized that she wasn't breathing. "Oh my God. I killed her!" She fled the crime scene. Someone saw Joann running away looking frantic, and they understood why as they went to Julia's dressing room. The police were called. Later, they found Joann, and charged her with murder. People all over the world were heartbroken when they heard the news of Julia's murder.

GOD'S REDEMPTION

Joann hated herself and was suicidal. She killed the person who she used to love and had nothing to live for. She was a widow and now would spend the rest of her life in prison. She was sentenced to life in prison and denied any chance of parole. Joann would look at the four walls of her cell daily. She would read books to pass the time and began reading different kinds of genres. One day, she read a book about Paul in the bible. She enjoyed his story. He was a murderer as well, but God forgave him. He gave him another chance in life. She felt hope come inside her and she prayed for the first time in life. "Dear Lord, I messed up big time. I am sorry. I made many mistakes. Can you forgive me?" When she prayed that prayer, she began to weep uncontrollably. This was the first-time reality set in. She realized how being envious of Julia resulting in her killing her. She was ready to move on with her life in prison and make her life one of purpose like Paul's. She began to study the ministry of Paul and began to attend Bible study. She got saved during a meeting one day. Joann allowed the Lord to heal her. Over time, Joann found herself serving in the Bible meetings and assisting ministers as they preached. Joann knew that she would never leave prison, so she spent the rest of her life spreading the gospel to her fellow inmates. She was comforted to know that God forgave her and that He loved her no matter what her past mistakes were. Many you made many mistakes, and you are envious of someone. You can be set free today.

Dear Heavenly Father,

I repent of being envious of others. Help me to discover my identity in you. Help me to realize the gifts and talents inside of me. Help me to understand that the person that I envied has a different assignment from me. I bind up insecurity, murder, rivalry, strife and envy in Jesus name. Lord, set me free today and do a work in my heart. Thank you for answering this prayer in Jesus' name. Amen.

CHAPTER TEN
Fear

BY ANSTRICE EPPS

Do you know that Fear is a feeling that can paralyze you from your destiny, purpose, and life? Merriam-Webster defines fear as an unpleasant concern, often strong emotion caused by an unawareness of danger and instant emotion; an anxious concern.[19] Fear is a gripping, destiny stopping feeling. This feeling stops you right in your tracks. When you want to go left or right, you end up not doing anything at all. Fear leads to instability and a lack of contentment which is the enemy of our faith. The Bible says, "That God has not given us the spirit of fear, but of love, power and a sound mind (2 Timothy 1:7 NKJV)." Fear cost me everything. Now, let's discuss the root of fear and how we can cause this spirit to take rule over our lives with its consequences.

CONSEQUENCES

1. Emotional Instability

We are given a clear directive (from God) that fear is a spirit. It's not of God. This feeling had me in chains for so long. I would shrink all the time. I walked around with my head hanging low with shame and self-condemnation because of fear. When God called me, it was during walking in a life of fear. Fear wasn't a feeling that I talked about. However, it would show. The Bible speaks that out of the heart flows the issues of life (Proverbs 4:23 NKJV). No matter how much we try to hide fear, it will flow out of us if it's there. Our actions and thoughts will shape our very lives. According to healthline.com, some emotions that fear can cause are feeling of impending doom, panic in social settings, difficulty concentrating, irrational anger, and restlessness.[20] If there is fear in our lives, it will stop what God wants to do through us. Until we push past this feeling, it will keep us locked in a jail cell longing for freedom. We can obtain freedom in Christ Jesus from fear.

2. Stops Progression

Fear that grips, stop, and shakes us from progression is not from God; it's from the enemy, Satan, himself. Fear can act as a leash around your neck. We can start to make some progress in our lives and then feel as if the collar of fear snatches us. Fear stops us from moving forward with the plans that God has in store for our lives. For example, fear of failure will prevent us from producing the things that God has in store for us.

Downloads that God has given us can be on pause because of the fear of failure.

3. Effects on the body

Fear produces anxiety, stress, worry, and nervousness. Some physical symptoms of fear are stomachaches, muscle tension, headaches, rapid breathing, fast heartbeat, sweating, shaking, dizziness, frequent urination, change in appetite, trouble sleeping, diarrhea, and fatigue.[20] Fear has some physical effects that many of us are unaware of or don't realize. According to the Bible Helps website, the physical effects of fear or the results on our physical anatomy are paleness of skin, high blood pressure, arthritis, and even blindness in some cases.[21] Though we may think this is just a feeling or short-term sickness, these outcomes can be long term issues. Having these symptoms from fear are spiritual issues that manifest in the natural. We shouldn't look at this as something to pass over and be inattentive to. Instead, look at from a spiritual standpoint, admit that we are dealing with this spirit, and get to the root of fear.

4. Stuns our Growth

Because fear is so gripping, it stops and stuns our growth and progression. Not just in life, but in the things of God. Fear prevents the purpose that God intends for our lives. Fear makes you want to quit, stop, and give up. Fear comes with self-sabotage; make us began to question ourselves and question what God has called us to do. Fear is an enemy to us when it comes to us growing in our walk with God and life.

Loss of time

Due to fear having a grip in our lives, it also causes us to have time loss, spent, and wasted. We lose time wondering what could of, should of and would have happened if we took upon that moment, or that opportunity when it presented itself. We spent time being terrified of what others would say about us, approve of what we're doing, and having the support of others. We wasted time in the moments that we cannot get back all because of fear. Now, there is a fear that is healthy for us to have in our lives. That fear is the fear of the Lord. Let's discuss this kind of fear that God honors.

In the fear of the LORD there is strong confidence, And his children will have refuge. The fear of the LORD is a fountain of life, that one may avoid the snares of death (Proverbs 14:26-27).

There are so many scriptures about having the fear of the Lord. Therefore, this fear, defined by Merriam-Webster, is described as having profound reverence and awe toward God. In other words, a great respect for God. This fear is necessary to have so that we won't go around thinking that we can do what we want to do and there will be no consequences. This fear is knowing that the eyes of the Lord go to and fro throughout the whole earth, to show Himself strong on behalf of those whose heart is loyal to Him (2 Chronicles 16:9 NKJV). So, you see, having this fear towards God, our Father is necessary to serve Him wholeheartedly. Now, we will talk about how I let fear almost trap me into not pursuing God's purpose for my life.

ANSTRICE'S TESTIMONY

I was filled with the Holy Ghost one day sitting on my couch listening to T.D. Jakes in 2015. After that day, I was never the same. Growing up in church was one thing, but knowing, feeling and encountering God for myself was another. God started to show me visions and dreams. In 2016, I had a vision that I was waving to a coliseum full of people as I was preparing to speak on stage. I had this vision in the middle of having dinner with two women. The vision stunned me so much that I froze on my goals for the rest of that year. God, how can you use me? Do you know my past? Do you know the sins that I have committed? Are you sure? Not me God, not me. I've done things that I'm not proud of. I've lied, tried to control outcomes, committed sins that I can't take back and been rejected. There is no way that You can use me. I'm too dirty God, just too dirty. At that time, I was full of shame and guilt.

We don't realize that God knew us before he formed or knitted us in our mother's womb (Jeremiah 1:5 NKJV). The Father already knew every bad thought, decision, mistake, and mishap that we would ever do or think about doing. He created us. He knew the things that we were going to do and meant all things to work for our good (Romans 8:28 NKJV). As I grew to know God's character, love, mercy, and kindness, I began to trust Him. I started to lean on His understanding and not my own (Proverbs 3:5-6 NKJV). This is a faith walk with God. If we could do it all by ourselves, why would we need God? For several years, I let the fear of what others thought about me, stop me from doing so many things that God had for me. So many times, I would be motivated to start something but never finish. In January 2017, God called me to start a blog, and he gave me the name "She Writes for God." I didn't know how to start a website or a blog, let alone, think that I could even write. I never thought that I had a desire to write.

GOD'S REDEMPTION

God's plan was opposite of what I had in mind for my life. However, I stepped out on faith and started the blog. God was testing my faithfulness and commitment to Him by starting this blog. I would be sitting in my living room, and He would give me the title of the message and the scriptures to support the messages that He wanted to convey. Doors started to open in 2018 after one year of having the blog. Then the opposition began to surface. Negative comments were made on social media. I experienced resistance from the people closest to me. God would send messengers to speak to me at work, at church, or at random every time I wanted to quit. We cannot let fear hold us back from what God wants to do in our lives. Fear robs us from us. Fear steals what God wants to give us. Fear blocks the blessings God has in store for us. Fear cost me time that only God can redeem. If we activated our faith and believed God over ourselves and people, imagine how far God would have us now. But, thank God that He redeems and restores lost or wasted time.

"So, I will restore to you the years that the swarming locust hath eaten, the cankerworm, and the caterpillar, and the palmerworm, my great army which I sent among you (Joel 2:25)." God is so merciful and gracious towards us that He restores, strengthens, and renews us as much as we need. Countless times God is ready to refresh us as much as we need to be refreshed. Fear cost me everything because time is something you cannot get back. However, time can be restored by the Father. The creator of all creation. For he is the author and finisher of our faith (Hebrews 12:2 NKJV). When we surrender our will and obey God, He will redeem the time lost, spent, and wasted out of His will. God will cause all things to work together for our good (Romans 8:28). Even our mishaps, mistakes, pain, and time wasted will still be used to glorify Him. I encourage you to let God into your hearts. Let Him do the work that is necessary to do His will. God never ask for us to be perfect and have it all figured out. God asks for us to say yes to His will. Now, let us pray to remove fear through the name of Jesus.

Father, we come before You repenting of all of our sins. We are repenting for having fear in our hearts. Perfect love cast out all fear (1 John 4:18). God, we invite your perfect love into our hearts, casting out all fear that is within us. For we know that you haven't given us a spirit of fear, but of love, power, and a sound mind (2 Timothy 1:17). We embrace the power, the love, and a sound mind that has been given by You. Father, we cast out all fear within our hearts, minds, and spirits. We know that our bodies are a temple of the Holy Spirit. We are not our own because we were bought with a price (1 Corinthians 6:19-20). Forgive us for sinning against our bodies and causing harm through fear in our temples. Heal anything in us that was damaged by fear. Remove the anxiety within us that is caused by fear. For you are God that heals us from all our diseases (Psalm 103:3). In the name of Jesus, we pray. Amen.

CHAPTER ELEVEN

Fornication

BY MELISSA PORTIS

Did you know that fornicating comes with consequences? According to Merriam-Webster, fornication means consensual sexual intercourse between two persons not married to each other.[22] When we sleep with someone who is not our spouse, we not only sin against ourselves but we also sin against God. We are to flee from the lust of the flesh and pursue righteousness (2 Timothy 2:22). I had to suffer the consequences of fornication in more ways than one. Being out of the will of God cost me everything! Sexual intimacy was created to be between husband and wife (Genesis 1). It was never intended for us to feed our flesh by "testing out the goods" or having multiple partners. You are opening yourself up to receiving spirits of people that your partner has slept with. This can also be a gateway to other unlawful acts, which may very well leave a person open to demonic possession. Mark 5:9 says, "Then He asked him, "What is your name?" And he answered, saying, "My name is Legion; for we are many." Despite what our flesh wants to do, we must practice self-control. To do that, we must know the word of God. Meditate on it day and night (Psalms 1:1-3).

CONSEQUENCES

Now that we know what fornication is let's discuss some of the effects. Having sex outside the will of God can lead to the following:

1. Unwanted pregnancies

John 10:10 (NKJV) says, "The thief does not come except to steal, and to kill, and to destroy. I have come that they may have life, and that they may have it more abundantly." God gave women a wonderful gift. An opportunity to conceive and bring life into this world. I know so many people who have fornicated, and as a result, they became pregnant multiple times. Not able to make clear decisions due to fear, thinking that their only choice was to terminate the pregnancies and others being forced by their partners.

2. STD's

Micah 6:13 (NKJV) says, "Therefore I will also make you sick by striking you, by making you desolate because of your sins." I have known people who have contracted STDs; running to the doctor repeatedly to get medication, and to stop the discomfort. I also knew someone who contracted an incurable disease that western medicine could not cure. That person is no longer here today.

3. Mental instability

Ephesians 6:12 (NKJV) says, "For we do not wrestle against flesh and blood, but against principalities, against powers, against the rulers of the darkness of this age, against spiritual hosts of wickedness in the heavenly places." Fornication will cause the enemy to torture your mind. I have known people to fall into a deep depression and even suicide. They became double minded and not able to make rational decisions.

4. Soul Ties

1 Corinthians 6:16 (NKJV) says, "Or do you not know that he who is joined to a harlot is one body with her? For "the two," He says, "shall become one flesh." I have known people to try to break free from wrong relationships repeatedly, but they just can't. Fornicating caused their souls to become one who gave the enemy permission to keep them in bondage. Fornication also gives the enemy permission to torment the person who wishes to break free. It may take several years or something detrimental to happen for a person to break the soul tie completely.

5. Manipulation

Romans 16:18 (NKJV) says, "For those who are such do not serve our Lord Jesus Christ, but their own belly, and by smooth words and flattering speech deceive the hearts of the simple." When someone fornicates, they become susceptible to being manipulated and believing lies. I have known people who were in relationships for years. They would pacify the person and tell them everything they wanted to hear. This was merely a sexual relationship. Even though the signs were evident, the nature of the relationship was only clear to the manipulator.

6. Rejection

Isaiah 53:3 (NKJV) says, "He is despised and rejected by men, A Man of sorrows and acquainted with grief. And we hid, as it were, our faces from Him; He was despised, and we did not esteem Him." I have known people to be ridiculed and outcasted by family and friends due to their promiscuous lifestyle. As a result, they became shameful, and the spirit of rejection manifested in their life.

7. Fear

2 Timothy 1:7 (NKJV) says, "For God has not given us a spirit of fear, but of power and of love and of a sound mind." The Bible clearly states that God did not impart fear into His people. The opposite of fear is faith. I have known couples that have decided to live with one another. They become sexually active, compromising their morals and values, only to prevent them from sleeping with someone else. I have seen this method fail in many people's lives. When you sleep with someone who is not your husband or wife, you are NOT putting your trust in God, but leaning to your own understanding.

8. Lust

2 Timothy 3:6 (NKJV) says, "For of this sort are those who creep into households and make captives of gullible women loaded down with sins, led away by various lusts." When you lust after someone, you open yourself up to deception which is one of the ways that the enemy comes in to plant seeds of confusion. For example, seeds of confusion such as thinking that lust is really love.

9. Sexual Addiction

1 Corinthians 6:18 (NKJV) says, "Flee sexual immorality. Every sin that a man does is outside the body, but he who commits sexual immorality sins against his own body." I have known people who have sought out prostitutes, due to their sexual addiction. It basically took over their lives and became a habitual act. According to the United Church of God, preoccupation is the mood or trance in which the mind becomes completely engrossed with thoughts of sex. This mental state creates an obsessive search for sexual stimulation.23

10. Generational Curses

Lamentations 5:7 (NKJV) says, "Our fathers sinned and are no more, But we bear their iniquities." I have known people who have gone through the same negative patterns and cycles as some of their family members. Such as all the women on one side of the family never being married or being barren. As a result of fornication or sin, this can cause these types of curses to pass on from generation to generation.

MELISSA'S TESTIMONY

Since we have covered the consequences of fornication, let me explain how it cost me everything. I've always had a desire to become a wife. Little did I know, I was going about it all wrong. Before I got saved, I always needed to be in a relationship with a man. I felt incomplete if I wasn't in one. I was a faithful girlfriend but also a fornicator. I had a high sex drive and demanded it on a consistent basis. I thought well if I'm in a relationship and not sleeping with multiple people then it was ok. I wasn't asking about his walk with God. I was only concerned if he was committed to me and if he was good in the bedroom.

Let's take a journey and explore one of my past relationships. I was with Chuck for several years who I thought was "the one." We spent a large amount of our time in the bedroom. This man had me wrapped around his finger: emotionally, physically, and mentally. We did just about everything together, but deep down inside I still felt lonely and incomplete. I always looked forward to being sexually intimate with him. It was like an adrenaline rush because it gave me a sense of security. I was comparing sex to love. I didn't ask for much, only for my flesh to be satisfied. Yet, I was looking for this man to marry me.

The holiday season came around, and I was confident he was going to pop the big question. Well, instead I received a message in my inbox from a woman stating she was pregnant by him. I immediately had a flashback of our past. I also was pregnant at one point with his child. We decided it wasn't the best time, so I terminated the pregnancy. I couldn't believe he had slept with someone else. I was so devastated. My body became cold and my fingertips numb. I kept thinking to myself, "When did he find time to do this?" A secular artist song continued to replay over and over in my mind. It was by Jazmine Sullivan, "Bust Your Windows.".. That's just what I had planned to do to Chuck's car. At this point, I was not thinking straight. Thank God I received a phone call from my best friend who prevented me from acting irrationally.

When I told him about the message I received, he confessed it was true but tried to deny the baby was his. The child turned out to be 99.99% his! I ended the "relationship" and decided to move on. I attempted to go back on social media, but it was very hard emotionally. I saw pictures of him, the baby, and the female together. Not to mention the phone calls I received from my friends asking if I had seen the photos. This was not the first time this had happened to me. Same situation different person. A demonic cycle of wrong relationships continued to enter my life. I shut down from the world and fell into a deep depression. Fornication cost me to have a lack of confidence. I felt as though I would never become a wife and that I was going to die alone. I had ultimately cursed myself by sinning against God. I had a constant mental battle of how I viewed myself. I felt worthless, miserable, unloved, and unimportant. I became lifeless and spiritually dead (Romans 6:23).

GOD'S REDEMPTION

You have witnessed how fornication caused me to make wrong decisions, develop false images of myself, and open doors to the enemy. Now I want to tell you about God's redemption. He tells us in His word in James 4:8 (NKJV), "Draw near to God and He will draw near to you. Cleanse your hands, you sinners; and purify your hearts, you double-minded." That's just what I did like never before. I drew closer to God and repented for my sins. The Lord has been trying to get my attention for years, and I was ready to be set free from the hands of the enemy. I was tired of the demonic cycles in my life. I needed a way to break free for good! I repented and surrendered my life to God, and my life began to change.

I stopped fornicating and began to study God's word, really engulf myself in it. Joshua 1:8 (NKJV) says, "This Book of the Law shall not depart from your mouth, but you shall meditate in it day and night, that you may observe to do according to all that is written in it. For then you will make your way prosperous, and then you will have good success."

I was ready to be made whole, so I decided that enough was enough! I needed to have the word of God in my spirit. To change my mindset and break the curses off my life, I knew I had to submerge myself in fellowship and intimacy with Him; through studying, praise and worship, and spending more time than the average in His presence. I became conscious of making sure I left no door open for the enemy to creep in. James 4:7 (NKJV) says, "Therefore submit to God. Resist the devil and he will flee from you.

At this point, I became captivated with a deep desire to be closer to Him. He became my comforter, and I rely on Him for all things. Matthew 5:4 says, "Blessed are those who mourn, For they shall be comforted." I knew His healing power. If He did it for others, I knew He could do it for me. Acts 10:34 says, "Then Peter opened his mouth, and said, Of a truth I perceive that God is no respecter of persons." I became Holy Ghost filled with the evidence of speaking in tongues. He also began to speak to me in dreams. He showed me people, places, circumstances, and situations that someone may have been going through. The Lord put a burden on my heart for prayer; waking me up at odd hours of the night (Isaiah 62:6). I've also experienced visitations, giving me peace and releasing His love upon me. This is now a lifestyle that the Lord has imparted in me.

I'm sharing my testimony to let people know that God is real. He loves you, and He's faithful. He'll deliver you from whatever is keeping you in bondage. 1 Corinthians 10:13 says, "No temptation has overtaken you except such as is common to man; but God is faithful, who will not allow you to be tempted beyond what you are able, but with the temptation will also make the way of escape, that you may be able to bear it." I became so hungry for the Lord, wanting to be in His presence; wanting to please Him. I've come a long way, and I know that God is not done with me. Even though friends have left, and relationships have ended due to my walk with Christ, I continue to show myself approved. Deuteronomy 31:8 (NKJV) says, "And the Lord,

He is the One who goes before you. He will be with you, He will not leave you nor forsake you; do not fear nor be dismayed."

The Lord has brought new friendships into my life and people of God who genuinely care about me and my walk with Christ. I don't have all the answers, but I know when I put Him at the forefront of my life, things began to shift and change in my favor. My mind is set free from thoughts that are contrary to the word of God. Compromising is no longer an option. The man that the Lord has for me is a man who lives by the word of God. He will love me just as Christ loved the church. Ephesians 5:25 says, "Husbands, love your wives, just as Christ also loved the church and gave Himself for her." I used to lean on my own understanding trying to figure out why real love was passing me by? Why relationship after relationship no one was made my husband? Why was I going through so much heartache? I had questions, and I needed answers. Well, it was because I hadn't fully given my life to the Lord. I wasn't committed to trusting Him. The Bible says in Psalms 37:4 (NKJV), "Delight yourself in the Lord and he shall give you the desires of your heart." I was delighting myself in people, things, and having idols. The key is to surrender and love on God completely with your whole heart. It also goes on to say in verse 5, "Commit your way to the Lord, Trust also in Him, And He shall bring it to pass."

Ladies, I'm here to tell you, sex does not keep a man, nor does it persuade him to marry you. It doesn't matter what kind of tricks you can do in the bedroom, that won't keep him either. If you desire marriage and have a call on your life stop living in sin and fornicating, ask the Lord for forgiveness and seek Him wholeheartedly.

Gentlemen, a Godly woman adds favor to your life which means she is a gift. She will add to the plans and purposes that the Lord has for you. Proverbs 18:22 says, "He who finds a wife finds a good thing And obtains favor from the Lord." If you're living in sin and fornicating, ask the Lord for forgiveness and seek him wholeheartedly.

Dear Heavenly Father,

I repent for fornication and all that I have sinned. You said in Romans 3:23, "For all have sinned and fall short of the glory of God." I give it all to You Lord, I surrender. I thank You for Your grace and mercy. The love You have for me cannot compare, Oh Lord. You are my rock and salvation. You have delivered me from myself and the enemy. I will forever love You and praise You. In Jesus' name. Amen.

CHAPTER TWELVE
Gluttony

BY KIMBERLY MOSES

Have you ever overeaten because the food was so delicious that you just wanted more of it? Many people overeat and eat the wrong foods. When someone overeats often, they may be considered greedy. Gluttony is another name for greedy people. Merriam-Webster defines gluttony as excess in eating or drinking; greedy or excessive indulgence.[24] A person who deals with gluttony will sit and eat a whole gallon of ice cream, a large bag of potato chips, and drink one liter of soda in one sitting. Proverbs 23:21 says, "For the drunkard and the glutton shall come to poverty: and drowsiness shall clothe a man with rags." Nothing good comes from gluttony, and it will cost you everything. Now that we have defined gluttony let's look at its consequences.

CONSEQUENCES

1. Sickness

Gluttony can make you sick. You may overindulge in sweets and pay for it later with some bathroom action. For instance, when I was a child, I ate a bunch of food on Easter. I had a big plate at my parent's house, then another plate at my friend's house, and some gumbo and ice cream at another friend's house. When I came back home, I ate some chocolate. I wasn't hungry when I ate all those plates, but I was greedy. Later, I was sick to my stomach. Also, gluttony can cause sickness long term. Many people are dealing with diabetes, heart disease, high cholesterol, cancer, and hypertension. Over time, you will gain weight if you aren't exercising. Obesity can affect your breathing and cause arthritis in your joint due to the excess weight.

2. Death

Gluttony over time can kill you. It's sad to see someone who has a heart condition and has a doctor's order to eat better but won't do it. I witnessed many people pass away because they took eating to the extreme. A famous rapper named Big Pun used to eat several buckets of fried chicken from KFC in one sitting. He is no longer here today. Another gentleman that I know personally, can't breathe because of excessive fluid on his lungs and heart. He is in and out of the hospital every few days. When he gets out of the hospital, he eats waffles with lots of butter and fried chicken on the side. My great aunt passed away because she ate a bunch of salty ham and collard greens on Thanksgiving.

She was obese and had high cholesterol. She knew she was supposed to watch her salt intake, but she didn't care. She died the next day.

3. Poverty

Gluttony will result in poverty because you are spending all your money on food. Imagine how big your grocery bill will be. You will just run through food just because it's around. Many people have saved hundreds of dollars annually by eating at home instead of eating out. The average household spends $3,008 on dining out.[25] That's more than what some people make in a month. Now that we covered some consequences of gluttony, let's look at how it can cost you everything!

PAUL'S STORY

Paul was a handsome man. A lot of women wanted to date him. He took pride in smelling nice and wearing the latest clothes. However, Paul had a problem. He loved food. He would indulge in significant portions of food. When his family would have dinner, He would always have the most massive amount on his plate. He would eat a third helping sometimes. He ate breakfast, lunch, dinner, and several snacks in between. He would wake up in the middle of the night and eat ice cream, cookies, or potato chips. Afterward, he would go to sleep. Over time, Paul gained an additional 80 lbs.

Paul's weight gain wasn't that obvious to some because of his height. However, the people closest to him noticed it in his face, arms, and torso. Paul loved Hawaiian Punch and Pepsi. Before he would go to work, he would stop by a convenient store and buy a gallon of either drink. He would drink the whole gallon before his shift ended. Paul did this for a month, until one day something unusual occurred. Paul kept going to the bathroom more than usual.

He was trying to finish up his assignment on his job but was having difficulty doing so. He kept stopping every 5 to 15 minutes to go back to the restroom. Around the 6th time doing this, his eyes became blurry. Paul couldn't see. He felt disoriented and stumbled out of the bathroom. Someone was passing by and saw him having trouble walking. They stopped and assisted him. They led him to a chair so that he could sit down. Then they called an ambulance. Paul was rushed to the hospital and diagnosed with type 2 diabetes or sugar diabetes.

After Paul was educated on diabetes and how to live with it but he didn't change. He was careless. He didn't wear socks on his feet like the doctor instructed and ended up getting a sore on his foot. The sore became infected. Paul had to return to the hospital for treatment. Paul wasn't compliant with his medicine. He wasn't on top of getting the prescription refilled. He always ran out of insulin and almost went into a diabetic coma several times due to his sugar being extremely high. The worst part is that Paul didn't exercise or change his eating patterns.

One day Paul ate a bunch of sweets, and his blood sugar increased. He went to take his usual dosage of insulin, but it wasn't working. His blood sugar wouldn't decrease. Instead of him going to the hospital to get treated he decided to wait it out and go the next day since it was late at night. Paul went to bed and woke up around 1:45 am. He knew something was wrong. He couldn't move one side of his body, and he was having a hard time seeing. He noticed he was drenched in sweat. He managed to pick up his cell phone and called 911. An ambulance was dispatched and took him to the emergency room. A CT scan was done. After his blood sugar was stabilized, the doctor's told Paul he had a stroke and was blind in his right eye.

GOD'S REDEMPTION

Paul spent several weeks in rehabilitation. He received excellent care from great staff. Each person was compassionate and seemed to care about him. Many of his nurses had one thing in common, their faith. Each one talked about their faith and the healing power of God. Some of them even prayed over Paul. Paul started to feel encouraged and wanted to know Jesus as well. A chaplain came to see him one day in the rehabilitation clinic, and Paul got saved. As time went on, Paul learned to talk and walk again. He was eventually discharged.

Paul wanted to know Jesus for Himself, and he was hungry for the supernatural. As he was scrolling on Facebook one day, he saw a flyer and noticed the word, 'healing.' It grabbed his attention. He realized that the healing service wasn't too far from him. Paul went that night to the healing service. Paul was amazed at the miracles that he was witnessed at the event that night. So, he went up for prayer and God restored his sight. He testified that he had a stroke about three months ago and lost sight in the right eye. He said, "I felt fire go into my eye and it felt like something lifted. Afterward, I could see. I covered my left eye up with my hand to confirm that I wasn't blind in the right eye." At that moment, everyone started praising God.

The Holy Spirit began to deal with Paul about his eating habits. Paul started to work out and ate healthier. Over time, He lost 82 pounds. He met a beautiful lady at the gym. Eighteen months later, they got married. He enjoys cooking healthy dishes for his wife and friends. You may currently be dealing with gluttony, but the power of God can set you free.

Dear Heavenly Father,

I give you praise, and I repent of being gluttonous. Lord, bless me to yield my appetite to you. I decree that I will no longer overeat. I decree that I will make better food choices. I decree that I will exercise. I decree that I will not die prematurely due to being greedy. Jesus, set me free. Strengthen and guide me to practice self-control. I crucify my flesh today in the name of Jesus.' Amen.

CHAPTER THIRTEEN
Guilt

BY KIMBERLY MOSES

Have you ever felt terrible because of something that you did or said? Many times, in life we may feel guilty because of the mistakes that we have made. When this occurs, we become filled with remorse and start reflecting on things we should've said or could've done which happens when we feel guilty. Guilt is the feeling of deserving blame especially for imagined offenses or from a sense of inadequacy; a feeling of deserving blame for offenses. It is also self-reproach.[26] Guilt will cause you not to value or appreciate yourself. Leviticus 5:4 says, "Or if a soul swears, pronouncing with his lips to do evil, or to do good, whatsoever it be that a man shall pronounce with an oath, and it be hid from him; when he knoweth of it, then he shall be guilty in one of these." Guilt can cost you everything! Now that we discussed guilt let's explore the consequences of it.

CONSEQUENCES

1. Condemnation

Guilt can cause the spirit of condemnation to set in. When this happens, the devil begins to torment your mind. He will keep reminding you of all your failures in life. He will whisper lies such as, "It's never going to work." "You aren't good enough." "You always mess things up." "You're stupid." Overtime, you will feel worse if you listen to the lies and start believing them. The word of God tells us that Jesus paid the price for our sins. When we get in the will of God, the devil can't condemn us anymore. Romans 8:1 says, "There is therefore now no condemnation to them which are in Christ Jesus, who walk not after the flesh, but after the Spirit."

2. Over Performance

Have you ever met someone that was over the top? They try too hard to fit in. They give too much for an assignment. They go an extra mile to do something when only one mile was required. Guilt will cause you to overperform. People will start to notice that your actions are extreme. Guilt will have you walking on egg shells and afraid to mess up again. There is no freedom in your life if you are consumed with guilt. If you are dealing with guilt, you might always feel that you must make up for your short comings and failures as another opportunity to get it right.

For example, a father hasn't been in his children's lives for about five years. He was feeling guilty for missing out on crucial moments in his children's lives; when they lost their first tooth, started walking, or began to talk. When he gets around his children, he spends money that he doesn't have to get his children to like and to love him again. He showers them with toys or whatever they want. He goes beyond what is necessary to make a statement of, "I brought you all of these nice things. Let me back into your life." This father is trying to cover up his guilt and make up for it monetarily. Every time he gets around his children, he feels like he must buy them something to make up for the lost time. His children aren't concerned about the fancy gifts. What they truly want is their father to stay in their lives.

3. Ruined Relationships

Guilt can destroy relationships for various factors. When someone is feeling guilty, they may withhold love. They may be afraid to express themselves because of what they experienced in past relationships. They might be afraid to open their heart to their loved ones and hold onto secrets. They may be hesitant to fully commit as well. Can you imagine how hurtful that is when your loved one is hurting because regrets are tormenting them, and they don't communicate with you? On the other hand, guilt can cause someone to cut off people and avoid them altogether. A guilty person might see that person they hurt as the source of their pain, and they don't want to face the mistakes that they made. As a result, they run from their problems. Can you imagine how hurtful it is when your loved one cuts you out of their life? Lastly, a guilty person might not be fully ready for a relationship because they keep bringing up their past into their current relationship. Bringing up your past into your present is a recipe for disaster. Now that we covered some consequences of guilt let's look at how it can cost you everything!

AMBER'S TESTIMONY

Amber was a beautiful, talented girl. She had big dreams and aspirations of traveling the world. She was focused on completing her goals in life until one day she met Mark. Mark was tall, handsome, and dark. She met Mark at Starbucks on her way to work. Every morning, she would go there and get her favorite latte. When Mark saw Amber, he wanted her. He built up the confidence and approached her. He asked for her number. Amber refused him, got her latte, and headed off to work. She thought she would never see him again.

Well the next morning, Amber runs into him again in Starbucks. Mark was very persistent. He asked for her number again as she waited for her pumpkin spiced-latte. Once again, Amber said no. She got her latte and headed off to work. Amber thought to herself, "This guy has some nerve. I don't have time to get involved with anyone." As the day ended, a new day began. Amber was on her usual routine. She wanted to get her latte and head to work without begin asked out on a date. When Amber walked into the door, she saw Mark again. She just chuckled because she said to herself, "This man will not take no for an answer."

Mark knew that he had to do something different this morning because Amber had already rejected him twice. He had been watching Amber the past two mornings and knew what her favorite drink was. He knew that she loved the cheese Danishes to go with her pumpkin spiced latte. So, he made a bold move. He ordered and paid for Amber's drink and Danish. He told the barista to hold it at the counter and give it to Amber when she is about to order. When Amber came into Starbucks a few minutes later, she saw Mark and shook her head. "This man just won't give up," she said underneath her breath. She walks past him and up to the counter. Before she could open her mouth, the Barista said, "Ma'am. The gentleman over there ordered and paid for this for you." She pointed to Mark.

Amber thought that was sweet. She took her latte and Danish and headed to the table where Mark was sitting, thanked him, and introduced herself. Mark and Amber had a quick chat and exchanged numbers before she headed off to work. She realized that Mark wasn't so bad. Every morning, Amber and Mark would talk at Starbucks, and she started to develop feelings for him.

Mark was a big distraction in Amber's life. At first, Amber refused to date Mark because she knew in her heart that she was trying to advance in her career which involved taking courses to get certified in management and hours of studying. Over time, Amber couldn't resist Mark's charm. He knew what to say to get to Amber's sweet spot. Amber was falling in love with Mark. They dated for a while and decided that they wanted to become more serious. They started having sexual relations with each other. They were engaged to be married shortly after. A couple of months went by, and Amber realized that she was pregnant.

"Oh no!" she thought. Amber didn't want children because she was career driven and about to go into the prime of her career.

She decided to abort the baby without telling Mark that she was pregnant with his child. On the day of her appointment, she lied to Mark where she was going. Amber didn't know that Mark had a cousin named Rita who worked as a house keeper at the clinic. Rita had seen Amber through social media, so she knew who she was. Amber never met Rita, so she didn't think anything about it as she passed by her as she mopped the lobby. Amber proceeded with the abortion and went home to rest. She took a few days off work and told Mark she wasn't feeling good.

A couple of days went by, and Rita sent Mark a text message. "Hey cousin, I saw your girlfriend at the abortion clinic the other day. Is everything okay?" When Mark read this message, his heart sank. He always wanted children. He felt betrayed because Amber didn't tell him about the baby. He was devastated. He called his cousin to get some details and assured her that all was well. He hangs up the phone feeling like a dagger was in his heart. He calls Amber and confronts her about the abortion.

At first, she tried to play it off, but she confessed everything. Mark broke off the engagement and never spoke to her again. Amber began to feel incredibly guilty. She lost the love of her life and murdered another human being. She messed up big time and fell into a deep depression. She realized how selfish her actions were and felt terrible inside. She tried to go back to work but was taunted at the sight of babies. Every time she saw a baby in the grocery store, television, or restaurant, it would trigger the guilt of her abortion. Sometimes, she would cry for hours because she missed Mark and wished she could've done things differently. Eventually, she got fired for missing too many days on her job. Guilt cost Amber everything.

GOD'S REDEMPTION

Amber hit a low point in her life. She let herself go, didn't style her hair anymore, and stopped dressing up. She would wear sweat pants and long T-shirts when she went out to run errands. One day as she went to Walmart to buy something for dinner, a lady came up to her in the parking lot. Her name was Monica, and she was an evangelist. She immediately discerned that Amber was dealing with guilt and depression. Monica had prayed earlier that day. God told her to go to Walmart to pray for someone who was feeling guilty for getting an abortion. Monica approached Amber with a smile full of the love of God. "Excuse me, ma'am. I don't mean to trouble you, but God told me that you had an abortion and you feel guilty about it. He said that He loves you. He has a great work for you to do if you accept His son in your heart today." When Amber heard these words, something broke within her.

She let out a big wail and bent over crying. Monica kneeled over with Amber right outside in the Walmart parking lot. Many people were stopping and concerned. Monica gently led them away by reassuring them that everything was okay. Amber was being delivered by the power of God. After she cried in the parking lot for about twenty minutes, she was able to talk. She gave her life to Jesus. Shortly after, she started attending

It Cost Me Everything

church with Monica. Amber went through the sanctification process for several years. When the time was right, God opened doors for her to be an advocate against abortion. Now Amber travels across the country telling her story and fighting against abortion. God blessed her to have a six-figure income. He even blessed her with an anointed minister, Anthony as her husband. Together Amber and Anthony work hard in their outreach ministry in their community.

You may have made terrible mistakes and feel guilty, but there is hope for you. As Amber got delivered, saved, and restored, you can too. God is calling you to do a great work. Will you accept Him today?

Dear Heavenly Father,

I come to you today and confess that I have been feeling guilty. I want to be free and not feel condemned about my mistakes. I repent Lord. I will get back in your will. I want to have a real relationship with you. I decree and declare that I will go through the deliverance and sanctification process. You tell me in your word that I am a new creature in Christ and old things are passed away. I will no longer believe the lies of the devil. Lord, you said that where your Spirit is there is freedom. I break guilt off me today in the name of Jesus.' Amen.

CHAPTER FOURTEEN
Idolatry

BY CAROLYN BOLER

We live in a day and time that someone always out shines, out numbers and overpowers each other to arrive at the top in the Market place of corporate America, medicine, and ministry. Whose or what altar are you worshipping? In this twenty-first century this is a question that we must ask. If we don't discern, we'll be worshipping new age, physics, witches, warlocks, root workers, instead of God, YAHWEH, Jehovah Jireh, Jehovah Sidkenu, Jehovah Rapha as the One True God.

In church history, humanity was not thankful for their portion of blessings and yearned to worship, praise, and serve images, serpents, people, and even one's self as a deity or "god" figure. It's within human nature to be competitive. Christians can gain healing and deliverance to walk in God's perfect will and blessings! According to Merriam Webster, Idolatry is the worship of a physical object as a god. It is the immoderate attachment or devotion to something.[27] Judges 2:11 says, "And the children of Israel did evil in the sight of the Lord, and served

Baalim." Idolatry is evil in the sight of God and it can cost you everything! Now that we know what idolatry is let's discuss its consequences.

CONSEQUENCES

1. Judgment

Whenever you disobey God's commands there will be judgment. Jeremiah 1:16 (ESV) says, "And I will declare my judgments against them, for all their evil in forsaking me. They have made offerings to other gods and worshiped the works of their own hands." God is not pleased with Idolaters. They will be judged. Judgment can sickness or getting attacked by natural disasters such as floods, fires, earthquakes, or more. Isaiah 65:3 (ESV) says, "A people who provoke me to my face continually, sacrificing in gardens and making offerings on bricks." When we practice idolatry, we are provoking the Lord to anger. For instance, Aaron made the Israelites a golden calf. The people began to worship it. This made the Lord so angry that he sent a plague (Exodus 32).

1 Samuel 15: 22-23 (NIV) says, "But Samuel declared: "Does the LORD delight in burnt offerings and sacrifices as much as in obeying the voice of the LORD? IT's a harmful thing not to follow through on God's Word and Command. Many have lost their lives and missed their season of Blessings. Behold, obedience is better than sacrifice, and attentiveness is better than the fat of rams. For rebellion is like the sin of divination, and

arrogance is like the wickedness of idolatry. Because you have rejected the word of the LORD, He has rejected you as king."

2. No salvation

People that practice Idolatry will not enter heaven. The reason is that Jesus is not their God and He is the only way to heaven. The Bible warns us multiple times that idolaters will spend an eternity in the lake of fire. Galatians 5:19-21 (ESV) says, "Now the works of the flesh are evident: sexual immorality, impurity, sensuality, idolatry, sorcery, enmity, strife, jealousy, fits of anger, rivalries, dissensions, divisions, envy, drunkenness, orgies, and things like these. I warn you, as I warned you before, that those who do such things will not inherit the kingdom of God." We are told to flee idolatry (1 Corinthians 10:14). It will only cause us sorrow (Psalm 16:4) which is what the enemy desires. He wants to destroy our lives by coming in as a counterfeit to the true living God. The result of idolatry is spiritual death.

2. Going & Looking Back

Whenever you have idolatry in your heart, it will cause you to go backward. Proverbs 26:11 declares, "As a dog returns to his vomit, so a fool returns to his folly." God delivered Lot's family and commanded them not to look back as the city was being destroyed. Genesis 19:17 (NASB) states, "When they had brought them outside, one said, "Escape for your life! Do not look behind you, and do not stay anywhere in the valley; escape to the mountains, or you will be swept away." Lot's wife looked back. Genesis 19:26 says, "But his wife, from behind him, looked back, and she became a pillar of salt." Philippians 13:13-14 (NASB) says, "Brethren, I do not regard myself as having laid hold of it yet; but one thing I do: forgetting what lies behind and reaching forward to what lies ahead, I press on toward the goal for the prize of the upward call of God in Christ Jesus." Idolatry will cause you to take your eyes off the Lord and place them on things that will have you to look back.

3. Deception

Idolatry can cause you to be deceived. Lucifer, the former musician leader in heaven was a head angel and he is known as Satan. He was cast out of Heaven with his demons because he saw and wanted God's Power. He wanted to control both good and evil. In the Hebrew, the name Lucifer is translated from the Hebrew word "Helel," which means brightness.[28] This designation, referring to Lucifer, is the rendering of the "morning star" or "star of the morning" or "bright star" which is presented in Isaiah. Isaiah 14:12-14 (NASB) says, "How you are fallen from heaven, O Day Star, son of Dawn! How you are cut down to the ground, you who laid the nations low! You said in your heart, 'I will ascend to heaven; I will raise my throne above the stars of God; I will sit on the mount of assembly on the heights of Zaphon; I will ascend to the tops of the clouds, I will make myself like the Most High." Deception makes you think that you can be like God.

2 Chronicles 26:16 (NIV) says "But, after Uzziah became powerful, his pride led to his downfall. He was unfaithful to the

LORD his God, and entered the temple of the LORD to burn incense on the altar of incense."

Zephaniah 1:4 says "I will stretch out my hand against Judah and against all against all who live in Jerusalem. I will destroy every remnant of Baal worship in this place, the very names of the idolatrous priests."

These are some of the implications of practicing idolatry. Let me tell you how idolatry cost me everything.

CAROLYN'S TESTIMONY

Idolatry cost me everything. Many years ago, I was employed at a Fortune Five Hundred Company. I desired and lusted for power and control. My career replaced prayer, ministry and time dedicated to God. On any given day, instead of listening to the voice of the Lord to fast, pray, read the Bible, minister, and Worshipping, I found my heart changing towards God. I was trying to accomplish my goals and desires! I felt that I had served God enough. It was time for me to excel in this earth. "I will get mines," I said. I had a super ego complex! The Spirit of the Lord was directing me to minister and be ministered to, but my spirit would cut off.

For a season I completely cut off God to gain what I thought was power and control. I did everything to try to get to the top. I would work long hours, connect to the right people, and become a "Yes Woman!" There was nothing too small or large that I would not do because I loved what I did! My 'yes' on a typical day would be running errands, typing memos, coming in early for presentations, and leading online workshops. I worked many hours and was not always paid. Sometimes I was tired, sleepy, sick with the flu and pneumonia. I crossed all my T's and dotted all my I's to attend to meetings! God was "calling" me to Himself and HIS Ministry for my life. He was not calling me to work in a Fortune Five Hundred Company. I told God, "I tell others about You. I am making six figures for myself and most of all for "the Kingdom!" Right, God was not having it!

I had my personal agenda. I was praying, fasting, paying tithes, offerings, going to church and prophetic Training. Yet my Spirit was still parched. I needed and desired more Word, worship, and time with God. I was warring within myself. I told God, "Yes. I'm giving You myself the altar." However, I still wanted my way. I just wanted to get corporate training.

I was running myself ragged. I thought that I would get a response back from the executive leadership or "Big wigs." I hoped that they would see my loyalty and promote me. Instead of being promoted, I was demoted and limited to the functions that I could do. Basically, I had to tend to my wounds, as if I was dead.

Because of this, I felt rejected, demeaned, overlooked, depressed and wanted to call it quits. I had nowhere else to go or do at the time. My hair fell out. I went on eating binges, then not eating at all. So, I took it one day at a time. I began to lay at the altar of the Lord for direction and repentance. I wanted my plans to matriculate beyond my present status. This season lasted about a year as a result of the doors that were open.

GOD'S REDEMPTION

The position that I interviewed for someone else got it! The Graduate Program was eliminated, and I was back to square one. The Lord was trying to keep me, though I was furious that I wasn't "Mrs. Corporate America!" A few years later, I later found out that half of the training department was cut due to a reorganization in the company. Lord, thank you for keeping me even when I did not want to be kept! You may want something badly, but it may not be the plan of God for your life. Anything that you place before God is an idol. He hates idols. Idolatry cost me everything, but God restored my life.

Dear Heavenly Father,

As the deer Paneth for the water, so my soul longs after You! YOU alone are my heart's desire and I long to Worship You!! I cry out to You, Oh Lord! Save us, set free us, and deliver us! Don't allow us to be the same! Thank You for loving Me! I believe that God sent His only begotten Son that I may have life! I believe that Jesus died and rose on the Third Day, that I may have life and more abundantly. I ask Jesus to become the Lord of my Life! I am saved. I ask the Comforter the Holy Spirit to come to be my Teacher, Paraclete, leader and intercede on my behalf.

I repent for serving, lusting, giving in, walking in, and worshipping idols on the altar of Baal, Baal Peor, pride, sex, pornography and power to be like God! I bind up the strong man of witchcraft from the Jezebel Spirit, which is fear, jealousy, that's trying to destroy the ministers and mouthpiece of God. I Destroy the altar of Lucifer, Leviathan, and pride. We renounce flesh and release love, healthy relationships, peace, and complete healing in Jesus Name!

Come out of the cave, men, and women of God! Come out of New Age! Come out of covetness, lust, adultery, and idolatry. Lord, I worship You, as a priest in my home. I humbly entering Your Holy of Holies Heavenly Father! Loose the Peace of God. We Humble ourselves at your feet. I lay on your Holy Altar. Make me again into Your image and likeness! I seek Your Face and worship You. I seal this prayer and deliverance session in the blood of Jesus. I expect growth. I desire in Your Word, prayer, and fasting to cast out anything that's not of you, Lord. This is my day of favor in Jesus' name. Amen.

IT COST ME ALL DECLARATIONS

1. I will put God first! I Seek first the Kingdom of Heaven. You are the Lord my God!
2. I will not serve Idols of New Age, Money, and Power!
3. I will have no other gods before YOU!
4. I will not make any graven images before YOU!
5. I will not waver between two opinions! The LORD is My God, and I will follow HIM.
6. I renounce the words and plans of the Astheroth, Jezebel, and Witchcraft Spirits. They will not take me out or my family before our time in Jesus Name!

7. I plead the Blood of Jesus!
8. I receive Your Holy Spirit, Protection, and Healing.
9. I renounce generational curses of sickness and disease. I decree health and prosperity.
10. I am the head and not the tail. I am above and not beneath!
11. I decree a new bloodline in my generation. I will not walk in the sins of my father and mother back sixty generations!!!
12. I decree a new walk! Those who served Baal: Sex, Power, and Money I Cast out In Jesus Name! I speak life, wholeness, and boundaries in God and life!
13. I decree A new talk!
14. I decree that it is my new day!
15. I decree that generational wealth is my portion in the Kingdom.
16. I decree that my ministry gifts will not be used for divination of sorcerers, physics, and evil tactics, but for God's use!
17. I will be a conduit for God to Use in this End Time!
18. I renounce legal rites, sexual acts, pornography, abortions, masturbation, fear begging, and laziness, from my ancestors back 3-4 generations
19. I release generational blessings, health, marriages, weddings, cleanliness, children, and work wealth in Jesus' Name.

CHAPTER FIFTEEN
Incest

BY KIMBERLY MOSES

All over the world family members are sleeping with one another. For instance, fathers are sleeping with their daughters and uncles are sleeping with their nieces which is incest. According to Merriam Webster, incest is sexual intercourse between persons so closely related that they are forbidden by law to marry.[29] Incest is against the law in most countries, and it is forbidden in the Bible. Leviticus 18:6-7 says, "None of you shall approach to any that is near of kin to him, to uncover their nakedness: I am the Lord. The nakedness of thy father, or the nakedness of thy mother, shalt thou not uncover: she is thy mother; thou shalt not uncover her nakedness." Incest can cost you everything! Now that you know what incest is let's talk about the consequences.

1. Disorders (Birth Defects)

A study was done on psychology today that showed the result of incest. 40% of the children born in incest were born with autosomal recessive disorders, congenital physical malformations, or severe intellectual deficits.[30] The Royal family has a congenital disability in their family due to inbreeding. Cousins marry each other. For instance, Queen Victoria's carried the gene for hemophilia, a blood-clotting disease caused by a defective X chromosome. She acquired the defective gene from both her parents because both of her parents were related to each other.[31]

2. Criminal Charges

Incest is punishable in most of the States in the U.S. Even between two adults who are related they can get up to five years to life in prison. The charges are similar with children. The people involved in incest will sometimes have to register as a sex offenders.[32] Being registered as an offender can hinder someone from getting employment, housing, and will also be on background checks.

3. Psychological Effects

Some mental issues come from incest. The participants are sexually attracted to one another, and they may need counseling or therapy to break the bad behavior. Children may need counseling to cope with physical and sexual abuse. Studies have shown long term mental issues for people who were involved in incest.[33] Incest is a very traumatic thing to go through, so they will need help, naturally and spiritually. Now that we have discussed the consequences of incest let's look at John's Story.

JOHN'S STORY

John grew up on a farm with his family. He had an awesome childhood. He learned agriculture and how to care for farm animals. His uncle Matt had a farm several acres away. John would go over to his uncle's farm sometimes to play with his cousins. John had a crush on his cousin Cindy. He thought everything about her was beautiful. As the years went by, John and Cindy formed an unusual relationship. They would hang out often, hold hands, watch the sunset, and they were each other's first kiss. They would sneak around to see each other and pretend like nothing was happening when they were around the rest of their family. John and Cindy were able to keep their relationship secret for several years.

One day, the truth was exposed. John's brother, Lawrence was suspicious of him, so he followed him one day. John wasn't aware that he was being followed because he had music blaring in his headset. Lawrence saw from afar Cindy and John meet in a secluded place in the forest. They greeted with a kiss and sat down on a blanket to have a picnic. Lawrence knew they were dating, and he ran back home and told his parents what he had just seen. John's parents immediately called Matt and his wife. They all were upset.

After John and Cindy finished their picnic, they each went their separate ways back home. When they arrived at their homes, they were greeted with disappointment. Their parents told them it was wrong to date their cousins. They said it went against their moral beliefs. John and Cindy both confessed their love for one another and didn't care what their family said. They decided to run away together the next time they were able to meet again. John was 16 and Cindy was 14. One night a few months later, they snuck out of their homes and met near some abandoned railroad tracks.

They traveled about 500 miles away into another small town. John and Cindy were able to get a job working on a family farm. They were able to rent a studio apartment. They weren't old enough to get married legally, but they promised to marry as soon as they were of legal age. They started being intimate with each other and shortly after Cindy got pregnant. When Cindy had the baby, she knew something was wrong. The baby was diagnosed with mental retardation. John and Cindy were heartbroken.

The authorities found out that John and Cindy were both underage. Child protective services got involved. Their family was separated, and they both had to return home to their parents. Their parents and siblings were glad to see them, but their actions also hurt them. Years later, John and Cindy did marry. Their child had slightly deformed facial issues. Every child they had a mental retardation diagnosis. However, their facial features weren't as bad as their first child. They were paying the price of their sins.

GOD'S REDEMPTION

John and Cindy ended up repenting before the Lord. They also repented for the grief they caused their families. They started to attend church regularly along with their three children. Their children were dedicated to the Lord. They also had many prayers concerning their mental diagnosis and irregular facial deformities. Over time, the Lord extended his grace, and a great miracle occurred. The facial deformities of each child improved drastically along with the mental diagnosis. Amazingly, each child was able to attend regular school and live a normal life. John and Cindy knew that they didn't deserve God's mercy and they were forever grateful.

If you committed incest, there is still hope for you. God's love can redeem. His love can set you free. Make a decision to allow Jesus on the throne of your heart. His ways are better than yours. His plan for your life is far better than yours.

Dear Heavenly Father,

I repent of my sins of incest. I renounce all sexual attraction with any of my family members. I renew my mind today with the word of God. I yield my spirit to you so you can do a great work in me. I give you my heart today. Lord, cut all ties of incest out of my life. Heal me and make me whole. Take me through the deliverance process so every inclination of incest in me can die by your power. Thank you for answering this prayer in Jesus' name. Amen.

CHAPTER SIXTEEN
Lust

BY KIMBERLY MOSES

Have you ever wanted something so bad that you did whatever it took to get it? For instance, you could have slept around to get a position or a promotion. The reason why this occurred is that you allowed lust for a position or promotion to overtake you. There are many people consumed with lust. Lust can't be quenched nor satisfied. Lust will cause a person to destroy their selves. It is defined as pleasure, delight, intense sexual desire, or an intense longing.[34] Galatians 5:16 says, "This I say then, walk in the Spirit, and ye shall not fulfil the lust of the flesh." The Bible warns us not to give in to temptation because when we do so, we are fulfilling the lust of the flesh. Lust cost me everything.

CONSEQUENCES

Now that we discuss what lust is let's cover some effects. If we don't get ahold of lust and receive deliverance, it will cost us the following:

1. Relationship Trouble

Many people don't consider the devastating effects that lust can have on relationships. Children are affected when their parents commit sexual sins or cheat on each other. The children carried emotional baggage of their parents' sins, and if they don't get delivered, then they end up lustful just like their parents. Friendships are destroyed because there will be no trust or boundaries. A person consumed by lust will steal positions, spouses, and businesses since lust is leading them to greed. They aren't concerned with anyone's feelings and nothing except the power of God will stop them from their destructive ways.

Amnon is an example of someone consumed with lust. He lusted after his sister Tamar. He ended up raping her (2 Samuel 13) which resulted in their brother Absalom killing him (2 Samuel 13:23-38). How can a brother rape his sister? One of the root causes is lust. Lust was something that their father David dealt with. Lust caused him to commit sexual sin with Bathsheba. Afterward, he set up her husband to be killed in battle (2 Samuel 11). The apple doesn't fall too far from the tree. Therefore, we must get delivered from lust so that spirit isn't passed down to our children.

2. Health issues

Lust goes further than sexual desires. We can lust after many things such as electronics, food, fame, wealth, etc. Lust can affect our health which works hand in hand with the spirit of gluttony. We have previously covered gluttony. Lust can result in you overeating and eating unhealthy foods that can lead to diabetes, hypertension, or heart attacks. Lust can result in someone getting STDs and not stopping having intercourse because they are so consumed with it. Lust can also open the door to allow other spirits in such as fear, death, and pride.

Two examples of lust causing health problems are Gehazi and Herod. The first is Gehazi who got leprosy because he was full of lust (2 Kings 5:27). He was also a liar and very corrupt. Gehazi saw an opportunity to get money and gifts, so he went after it despite the cost. He witnessed his master Elisha pray for Naaman's healing of leprosy. Naaman wanted to pay Elisha for the healing he received by offering him many gifts. When Elisha declined those gifts, Naaman left. Gehazi followed him, and Naaman gave him silver and clothes. When Gehazi returned, he lied to his master where he went. However, Elisha knew by the spirit of God and cursed him (2 Kings 5). Naaman's leprosy transferred to Gehazi. He didn't have to have health problems, but lust was the root of it.

The next example is King Herod, who was an evil King. He wanted all the fame, success, and no competition. He was bloodthirsty and lusted for power. He tried to go against the will of God and put out a wicked decree where all male children in Bethlehem under the age of two to be slaughtered (Matthew 2:16). His plans failed, and an angel of the Lord struck him, worms ate him, and he died (Acts 12:23). Worms eating you is considered a parasite. Parasites feed on flesh. They take all nutrients from the host or the person where they reside. Parasites can lodge in the lungs, gut, brain, heart, or other organs. Many people in impoverished countries die from parasites quite often. King Herod didn't have to die from health problems, but lust became his downfall.

3. No salvation

Today, many people are deceived. There is a doctrine of devils that states, "I will go to heaven because I am a good person." Jesus is the only way to heaven. He told us that no one could go through the Father except through Him (John 14:6). He set an example by which we are to follow (John 13:15). Jesus didn't have a lust issue. The bible is very clear that lust leads to spiritual death which results in eternal damnation or hell. James 1:15 says, "Then when lust hath conceived, it bringeth forth sin: and sin, when it is finished, bringeth forth death." You cannot enter heaven living un-righteously. Consider the following scriptures.

Know ye not that the unrighteous shall not inherit the kingdom of God? Be not deceived: neither fornicators, nor idolaters, nor adulterers, nor effeminate, nor abusers of themselves with mankind, nor thieves, nor covetous, nor drunkards, nor revilers, nor extortioners, shall inherit the kingdom of God. --1 Corinthians 6:9-10

4. Guilt

Have you ever messed up or sinned and felt horrible the next day? This is the aftereffects of lust and any sin. If your conscience is not seared or given over to a reprobate mind, then you will feel guilty. You might feel guilty for cheating, lying, fighting, stealing, or whatever after you finished. Lust will cause you to be overwhelmed with hot burning passion concerning the thing or person you desire. The enemy loves to blind us with lust so he can condemn us afterward. Condemnation doesn't come from God (Romans 8:1). Once condemnation sets in, then the enemy will further torment our minds. When this occurs depression, suicide, and a host of other spirits come in.

KIMBERLY'S TESTIMONY

Now that we have covered the consequences, let me tell you how lust truly cost me everything. Years ago, I was full of lust. I was selfish, and I often neglected my family at the time. I didn't know how to love others because I was so self-centered. I was married to my career and school. My first marriage was falling apart all because I was full of lust. No matter what my husband did for me, it wasn't good enough. I only focused on the negative things that he did. I didn't appreciate the hard work that he did for our family. Over time, we grew distant, and when an opportunity arose, I committed adultery. I remember that I surrendered my willpower over to the spirit of lust. Lust consumed my thoughts, and instead of casting it down, I ponder on it more. I could feel the spirit of lust consuming me at the time. It went through my whole body, and I didn't care about the things of God anymore. I just kept sinning and sinning. Each time became easier. One day, I found out that my first husband was also committing adultery and that just added fuel to the fire. I was on the road of destruction. Sinning was like a drug, and I couldn't stop no matter how bad I wanted too.

I remember having nervous breakdowns. I lost the peace that I carried previously for many years. Many people don't realize that God gives you peace that surpasses all understanding (Philippians 4:6) when you get saved so this is the peace that I carried until I sinned. I began to suffer from anxiety, and it was a five-year battle for me to get delivered from that spirit. I couldn't eat in public. I couldn't ride in the car with people. I couldn't meet new people without feeling sick to my stomach. I was afraid to leave my house and when I did, I would have panic attacks. The worst of part of this story is that I went through a divorce. I lost my house. My top credit score was non-existed because I was up to debt to my eyeballs. I hurt my family and children by my actions. Lust cost me everything!

GOD'S REDEMPTION

When I was tormented, believe it or not, I wanted to stop sinning. I didn't know how to stop. I would feel guilty because it seemed like I was always messing things up. I was tired of hearing the devil telling me how much of a failure I was. I was also tired of hearing him tell me how much he hated me and why don't I kill myself. I was struggling, and I was at the end of my rope. I did all that I knew how to do. I knew that I couldn't stop sinning on my own, so I cried out to God in my struggle. "Lord, please help me! I want to get back right with you! I want to stop sinning against you!" My prayer caused the Holy Spirit to be stirred up inside me again. I had suppressed and neglected Him for many months, but after this prayer, things began to change. I honestly meant those words in my heart.

The Holy Spirit began to give me instructions. He ordered me to block the person who was causing me to sin. I had to change my phone number. Since the person worked with me, they began to harass me while I was working. They wouldn't take no for an answer. I would avoid this person in every way. Since they wouldn't leave me alone, I believe that God allowed this person to get fired. Now that the person was removed, I could focus more on Jesus. I was a broken soul. I had many demons, and I needed deliverance. I started attending church on a regular basis. I stopped watching certain movies, and T.V. shows because they were planting seeds of lust inside of me. I started reading and studying my bible. God began to restore the joy of my salvation (Psalms 51:12) back.

I got my prayer life back, and the best part is that the peace of Jesus was restored in my life. Deliverance was a slow process, and it took around five years. I suffered and learned obedience through the things that I suffered just like Jesus (Hebrews 5:8). I learned to obey God in everything, and no matter how much I was tempted to sin, I said, "No. It's not worth it because it will cost me everything!" Over time, God gave me the wisdom to walk uprightly. He took my scarlet red stains of sin and made them white as wool (Isaiah 1:18). God gave me a second chance in life. He anointed me to set the captives free! If you messed up and want deliverance from lust, then pray from your heart. God will hear you and help you just like He did for me. Pray this prayer to help you on your journey.

Dear Heavenly Father,

I come before you. I confess that I am full of lust and I need your help! I am tired of sinning, and I want to be set free! I genuinely repent of my sins. Lord, strengthen me to live right. Bless me to go to church, read the bible, pray, and fast. Draw me nigh to you. Let the anointing come upon me and destroy every yoke of lust off my life. I humbly ask you to take me through the deliverance process today in Jesus' name. Amen.

CHAPTER SEVENTEEN
Lying

BY KIMBERLY MOSES

Many people are bound by lying. They lie about the simplest things such as their age, weight, experience, taxes, etc. Over time, they are nothing but a compulsive liar. It is easier to tell the truth than to tell a lie. If you tell the truth, then you will be free. However, if you tell a lie, then you must tell more lies when the first lie gets exposed for being false. According to Merriam-Webster, a lie is to make an untrue statement with intent to deceive. It also means to create a false or misleading impression.[35] The Bible tells us that God hates lying lips. Proverbs 12:22 says, "Lying lips are abomination to the Lord: but they that deal truly are his delight." Lying can cost you everything!

CONSEQUENCES

Now that we know what lying is let's discuss the implications.

1. No Salvation

Lying is one of the seven abominations that the Lord hates (Proverbs 6:16-19). How can you enter eternity to be with the Lord if you don't belong to him? Liars belong to the devil which is a bold statement and doesn't include someone who lied before and truly repented. This statement is about a person who is a compulsive liar. They don't walk in the truth of God, but they walk in deception. They spread lies and causes corruption in people's lives.

Ye are of your father the devil, and the lusts of your father ye will do. He was a murderer from the beginning, and abode not in the truth, because there is no truth in him. When he speaketh a lie, he speaketh of his own: for he is a liar, and the father of it.-- John 8:44

Liars will go to hell. They will be judged for every lie they tell (Matthew 12:36).

But the fearful, and unbelieving, and the abominable, and murderers, and whoremongers, and sorcerers, and idolaters, and all liars, shall have their part in the lake which burneth with fire and brimstone: which is the second death.-- Revelation 21:8

2. Broken Relationships

Imagine finding out that everything that your spouse told you was a lie? How would you feel? You would probably feel betrayed and like you are married to a stranger. Would you stay in the marriage and fight for it? Would you walk away? It would take the grace of God to work through all the rough patches. If you aren't honest in your relationship, then there will be no trust, hurt feelings, and a lack of respect. It will be hard to work or be around someone that you don't trust. It would also be hard to communicate with someone that lies about everything. Lastly, it will be tough to respect someone like this because all you could see is that they are a liar. It would take the mercy of God to put love in your heart for them to keep them lifted in prayer for their deliverance.

A froward man soweth strife: and a whisperer separateth chief friends.-- Proverbs 16:28

3. Jail

Lying under oath is considered perjury. According to Cornell Law School, someone can get up to 5 years of jail time for committing perjury.[36] It is not worth risking freedom to lie about something when you just could've told the truth. There is punishment for liars. There was punishment in the bible for being a false witness. The priests or judges judged the false witnesses. The judgment sometimes resulted in death (Deuteronomy 19:16-19).

A false witness shall not be unpunished, and he that speaketh lies shall not escape.-- Proverbs 19:5

A false witness shall not be unpunished, and he that speaketh lies shall perish.-- Proverbs 19:9

Now that I have discussed the consequences of lying, I will tell you a story about how lying can cost you everything.

PASTOR KENNY'S TESTIMONY

Pastor Kenny was an anointed man who God called at a young age. He was hungry for the things of God, so he decided to do something drastic. He went on an eighty-day fast which resulted in a closer relationship with the Lord. God began to open doors for Kenny. He traveled to many nations and people were in awe of his gift of the word of knowledge on his life. The reason is that they never saw anything like it before. As the request of preaching engagements increased, He lost the intimacy that he once had for God. Before his busy schedule, he used to spend time in prayer, worship, and reading the bible. Over time, he did these things less frequently. He stopped spending time with the Lord.

When the word of knowledge came forth in his services, he got caught up in the praises of people. As time went on, Kenny became prideful. He started down talking his staff, and he started to sin against God. Several accusations came out against him, but one scandal cost him his influence. He did a service where thousands of people gathered in attendance. People travel all over the world to get to this event. He gave a list of prophecies. He got the prophecies from a well-known psychic. His predictions matched exactly word by word to the psychic's prophecies. Someone who followed both his ministry and the psychic, made a video clip. The video compared Kenny's prophecies to the psychic's predictions. The video showed how Kenny was lying. It also showed that the psychic gave the predictions first. The sad part is that none of those prophecies came to pass.

When the scandal broke out, Kenny tried to lie about it. He lied and lied some more. Each of his lies unraveled, and the truth was revealed. He stole prophecies from a psychic to get people to like his ministry. He felt pressured to prophesy, and he wanted to impress the people. Many people in the church were hurt, and it did much damage. People began to shun prophets because of Kenny's actions. The doors of influence that he once had started to diminish. Kenny received fewer invites to speak at churches. His following on social media decreased significantly. His friends walked away. He was marked as a diviner in the church. He lost his businesses, houses, endorsements from companies and ministries. Lying cost Kenny everything.

GOD'S REDEMPTION

Kenny had to humble himself and repent publicly. He came forward and told the church that he missed it. He told the church that he stole the psychic's prophecies. He apologized for his wrong actions. For months, he didn't preach. Instead, he sought the Lord as he did in the beginning. He fell back in love with Jesus. He realized that he didn't always have to prophesy. He didn't allow anyone to put pressure on him either. His messages changed, and he became more Christ-like. Over time, God began to restore his ministry. Some influence that he once had returned. Doors began to fly open for him to travel and preach the gospel. If you have lied and hurt people, there is hope for you. If you have lost opportunities, people, and possessions God can bring restoration into your life. You may have lost everything, but God can give you truth another chance by His grace and mercy. Confess your sins, repent, and pray for the Lord's strength.

Dear Heavenly Father,

I come to you today and confess that I have a lying spirit. I have hurt people and caused a lot of pain. I repent. Please deliver me today. Get to the root of the issue within my heart. Bless me to walk in and be honest from this day forth. Give me the strength to do and say the right things. Lord, I ask you to develop my character, so that I can produce the fruits of the Holy Spirit. Your word tells me that the Holy Spirit is the spirit of TRUTH. Lead and guide me. Wash me in your blood today in Jesus' name. Amen.

CHAPTER EIGHTEEN
Molestation

BY DEWANDA ANN SAMUEL

For some who experienced childhood sexual abuse like molestation, it can rob you of your life. It's like a thief that comes in the night and steals all your valuables leaving you vulnerable. This heavy dark secret will cost you everything. But sometimes, there are these rare moments in time, when something triggers the memories of this dark secret. As a result, you began to feel defenseless and weak, so your guard comes down, and you decide this time, I am going to scream for help. This time, I am going to raise my voice, and I am going to tell someone—it cost me everything.

The weight of memories, the elusive emotions connected to this terrible experience had derailed my childhood and brought it to screeching stop. However, as you start to tell your story by revealing these experiences to people that you trust, you hope for compassion and understanding. But instead, you are victimized and abused again with the harsh questions. Unexpectedly, you are hit with another blow causing your life to come to a halt.

Now your mind is racing about thoughts of what is worst, the act of the sexual abuse you experienced or the mental abuse and rejection you received from the people that you love and trust.

The term sexual abuse covers a wide variety of inappropriate sexual behaviors and actions.[37] More specifically, the dark secret of molestation (i.e. sexual abuse) has damaging traumatic effects on many lives. Molestation is defined as to harm someone through sexual contact: to touch someone in a sexual and improper way.[38] Further, the bible talks about sexual immorality which is unlawful sexual intercourse, molestation which is similar but has a different name and different connotation that falls within this definition.

Galatians 5:19 (NAS) says, "Now the deeds of the flesh are evident, which are: immorality, impurity, sensuality, idolatry, sorcery, enmities, strife, jealousy, outburst of anger, disputes, dissensions, factions, envying, drunkenness, carousing, and things like these, of which I forewarn you, just as I forewarned you that those who practice such things shall not inherit the kingdom of God."

Not to mention, statistics show about one in ten children will be sexually abused before their 18th birthday.[39] Also, about one in seven girls and one in twenty five boys will be sexually abused before they turn eighteen.[40] As you can see, the numbers concerning child sexual abuse (i.e. childhood molestation) are high, and there is a probable chance it can happen in your family.

CONSEQUENCES

As a result of molestation, the consequences of it can ruin lives. As seen in Psalm 51:5 it declares, "Behold I was shapen in iniquity and in sin did my mother conceive me." Iniquity and sin have severe consequences according to the word of God. Molestation is an example of an act of iniquity. It is a wicked act committed by an individual against an innocent child victim. A person who experienced molestation will go through tremendous emotional, physical, psychological and social trauma in their lives. Sadly, molestation and its consequences have negatively shaped and deformed the lives of many individuals.

1. Emotional and Mental health problems

2nd Samuel 13: 12-13, 18-19 (ERV), illustrates when Tamar said to Ammon, "No brother! Don't force me to do this. Don't do this shameful thing! Terrible things like this should never be done in Israel! I would never get rid of my shame, and people would think that you are just a common criminal...Tamar was wearing a long robe with many colors. The king's virgin daughters wore robes like this. Tamar tore her robe of many colors and put ashes on her head. Then she put her hand on her head and began to cry." We see in the life of Tamar as a victim of sexual abuse caused by her brother. She knew this was an act that would bring much shame.

Shame interrupted and devastated Tamar's life as the "King's virgin daughter." Also, this shameful act drove Tamar into a state of dishonor, unworthiness, and shame. Whereby she tore her colored robe and put ashes on her head as a sign of mourning. Individuals who experienced sexual abuse live with much shame rooted in their soul. The weight of it causes them to live a lie making them believe that they are unworthy. It prevents them from living and being who they were called to be. Consequently, they feel like they can't be their authentic selves.

2. Obesity and Eating disorders

Obesity and eating disorders are more common in women who have been abused sexually during childhood. Middle aged-women who were sexual abused as children were twice as likely to be obese when compared with their non-abused peers. In addition, twenty-one-year-old women who were sexually abused as children were four times more likely than their non-abused peers to be diagnosed with an eating disorder. Philippians 3:19 (NIV) states, "Their destiny is destruction, their god is their stomach their glory is in their shame. Their minds are set on earthly things."

Proverbs 25:16 (NASB) declares, "Have you found honey? Eat only what you need. That you not have it in excess and vomit it." The effects of molestation have a way of altering how we consume our food. Some individuals eat in excess to numb the pain or suppress the memories. Research shows that 57,000 women found that those who experienced physical or sexual abuse as children were twice as likely to be addicted to food.[41] The soul is the container of the mind, will, and emotions. A mind that is not renewed in Christ Jesus will find its way of coping with problems, pain, hurt, and all negative feelings. God desires to heal, renew our minds and emotions from all hurt, trauma, pain, suffering, and all other negativity. I have seen individuals who experienced childhood sexual abuse use food to medicate deeper rooted issues in their soul ---the outcome of having an unhealthy desire for food ended up destroying God designed destinies. However, if we follow the wise instructions in the following verses, we will not be counted among the gluttonous and the drunks.

Proverbs 23: 20-21 (NASB), "Do not be with heavy drinkers of wine or gluttonous eaters of meat. For the heavy drinker and the glutton will come to poverty and drowsiness will clothe one with rags."

3. Sickness and Infirmity

Many who are sick are searching for the root cause of their illness, sickness, and infirmity. They may be surprised to find that there is an emotional problem that has manifested in their bodies. Everything good or bad in our lives starts as a seed and over time these seeds take root in our lives. Bad health has a root. For instance, Hebrews 12:15 (NASB) says "See to it that no one comes short of the grace of God, that no root of bitterness springing up causes trouble, and by it many be defiled."

Sicknesses such as cancer, stroke, and aneurysm have a root in bitterness. Consequently, survivors of childhood sexual abuse have more minor health conditions and they are at a higher risk for more serious diseases as well. Adults with a history of childhood sexual abuse are 30% more likely than their non-abuse peers to have a serious medical condition such as diabetes, cancer, heart problems, stroke or hypertension.[40] Victims must deal with the root problem of their childhood sexual abuse. Jesus has the ability and power to lay an ax to the root of bitterness, bringing healing to a person's soul and body.

Acts 8:23 (NASB) says, "For I see that you are in gall (i.e., poison) of bitterness and in the bondage of iniquity." A person who has been molested can have a gall of bitterness rooted in their soul and heart because of what happened to them. The gall of bitterness is very harmful to your body and soul. Our soul and what occurs in our body are connected. 3 John 1:2 (NIV) says, "Dear friend, I pray that you may enjoy good health and that all may go well with you, even as your soul is getting along well." If our soul is sick so are our bodies. Victims of molestation who live with a damaged soul will result in poor health.

4. Sexual Immorality

People today have an insatiable appetite for sex. Everywhere you turn sex is advertised in unsuspecting places such as food commercials. It is now even introduced in innocent children shows and games. There is an intrusive sex culture at work in our society that goes against the biblical laws of God concerning sex. Sex within the proper confines of marriage is acceptable by God. Hebrews 13:4 (NIV) says, "Marriage is pure before God. He will judge the adulterers and all the sexually immoral." Sexually immoral individuals will pay a great price in the end. In like manner, victims of childhood molestation can live a promiscuous lifestyle. Sex is introduced to these victims early in their childhood at no fault of their own. Now they are left with these sexual desires because of this sin of molestation. So, as they grow older, they are pulled in into sexual immorality. God is a merciful God, and He desires to bring liberty to those who are held captive to sexual immorality (i.e., Sin). Jesus shed His blood and died so that those who are bound by sexual immorality, they can be free. "...If the Son makes you free, you will be free indeed (John 8:36, NASB)." Equally important, 1 Thessalonians 4:3 (NASB) states, "For this is the will of God, your sanctification, that is, that you abstain from sexual immorality."

DEWANDA'S TESTIMONY

As an illustration of the consequences of childhood molestation, my testimony will show you the high cost I paid. As a young child, I lived in a large family. I was the middle child. There were three boys and four girls. Three of the older children lived between our house and their maternal grandmother's house. My father wasn't their biological father. Our home environment was dysfunctional. My mother was an alcoholic. My father would argue and beat my mother. He drank as well. But both of my parents worked hard, and we were considered a middle-class family. Also, our home was void of Jesus. I thought of myself as a daddy's girl. I would follow him everywhere. Growing up as an eight-year-old child I was quiet and (i.e., introvert), yet active. I used to love to dance. I was a standout smart kid who made honor roll and student of the month.

Unfortunately, that all change on that dreadful day when my older brother molested me. I asked myself, Why me? Why did he seek me out? I had three other sisters who were in the home. It was just like the enemy roaming around seeking whom he may devour (1 Peter 5:8). The enemy desires to plant his evil seeds early in a person's life. The enemy succeeded to sow confusion, depression, stunted my social development, gave me inferior complex towards men, made me promiscuous, and cause lust, perversion, shame, guilt, and anger in an eight-year-old girl.

The effects of the molestation quickly manifested in my life. I began to withdraw and isolate myself. I wasn't interested in being an exceptional student anymore. Negative feelings and thoughts were overtaking me, especially shame. My grades were failing. My name disappeared off the honor roll list just like my dreams. My life was a blur. But I remember as a young child I found a Bible. I would put this bible under my pillow, hoping that it would give me peace.

In my high school years, I was looking for love in all the wrong places. I thought having sex with my boyfriends proved that they love me. I would readily submit to their desires. I didn't understand my value; my soul and heart were wounded. At this point in my life, I was surviving and not living my life as a teenager. I remember one day in band, Mr. Hanson, my band teacher said to me, "Smile, where is that beautiful smile?" He and many others didn't know about my dark secret of molestation and how it took my smile away. At the same time, my home life wasn't any better. I couldn't tell my mother or dad about what had happened to me. The weight of molestation was heavy, and it cost me moments in my childhood that I couldn't relive.

"First comes love, then comes marriage, then comes the baby in the baby carriage." This was a famous childhood song we would sing on the elementary playgrounds. Well, my life was opposite of this song because I was pregnant in my last month in high school. I was a seventeen-year-old who walked across the stage and graduated pregnant with my first child. Marriage came. Two more babies were in the carriage, but there was no love. Now I was responsible for three babies who needed my love, care, and support.

Surprisingly I was able to love and protect them as a mother should. I guessed I discovered my maternal instinct. But as an adult, I still wasn't healed from the emotional and psychological damage from the molestation that I had experienced. I was stuck in my soul. It was tormenting me at the same time. I was trying to live my life as a single mother of three children. I was a young woman who had low self-esteem, with a dose of jealousy, anger, and shamefulness. I didn't know my worth. At times I was depressed. My childhood sweetheart, the father of two of my children, wanted to be a family. So, we decided to get married. I thought my life was good now because someone chose me. But that came to an immediate halt when I found out that my ex-husband was cheating.

I was deceived by the fantasy. I was still "messed up." I was emotionally stuck. So, I turned to food for comfort. Now, my physical body was being affected by the negative emotions rooted from the molestation I had experienced and from the infidelity caused by my ex-husband. The emotional and physical stresses weighed me down and held me hostage. So, I turned to my ex-husband for comfort and support even after his infidelity. I decided to tell him about what I experienced as a child.

However, I didn't receive a warm, loving or compassionate response from him. Instead, he responded with "Who told you to be messed up?" It was cold and harsh coming from a man that I loved. I realized that day I was married to the wrong man and that I needed help. Being a victim of molestation affected my life. More specifically, it robbed me of my emotional and psychological wellbeing in my relationships, dreams, identity, and physical health. My soul was crying out for help.

The Bible declares in Psalm 46:1 (NASB), "God is our refuge and strength, a very present help in trouble."

GOD' REDEMPTION

My life needed help and deliverance. What I was doing, or lack thereof was not helping, and it certainly was not working. But I found relief. One day I heard a lady praying fervently in an apartment above me, and I wanted what she had. This woman of God led me to Christ. I received and felt the saving grace of Jesus in my heart. I wanted more. I wanted my life back and everything God had for me.

I was running on empty for so long and living a confused life. I wanted Him to fill me with His Spirit. "Blessed are those who hunger and thirst for righteousness, for they will be filled (Matthew 5:6, NIV)." God was faithful. He filled me with His Spirit and with the evidence of speaking in tongues. Now, I had a new life in Christ Jesus and the power to live my best life; my authentic life. Jesus came into my heart and began to heal all the damaged areas within me. He removed the guilt and shame. He restored my identity. Slowly my anger was transformed into peace and love. The depression was transformed into joy. The oppression was transformed into freedom.

My mind was transformed into the mind of Christ. "Therefore, if anyone is in Christ, he is a new creation, old things have passed away; behold all things have become new (2 Corinthians 5: 17)." My life was new in Jesus, and I had the power of the Holy Spirit to live right. I got deep in the word of God and prayer was my life source. Consequently, I started making positive choices. I chose to have joy in my life. I began to see myself as God sees me. I practiced patience and the love of God. I consecrated my life by fasting. My life was turning around for the good. Indeed, He [God] has restored my soul (Psalm 23:3).

Dear Heavenly Father,

I repent of all my sins, and I turn to you God. I confess I have done wrong. I have been angry. I lacked love for others and patience. I sinned against You Father. Now, God, I release all the pain, molestation, shame, depression, anger, rage, hate, and confusion. My body, heart, and soul belong to you, Jesus. All the times I sinned against my body, forgive me, Jesus. Purge me with your Blood Jesus. Lord, take every negative feeling away, such as feeling unloved, loneliness, sadness, guilt, and shame. I give you my wrong motives. Clean me up with your Blood Jesus.

Fill me Lord with Your Holy Spirit, love, peace, and joy in Jesus' Name. Amen.

CHAPTER NINETEEN
Perversion

BY ZOLISHA WARE

Did you know that perversion is the enemy's greatest secret weapon used to destroying humankind? The secret weapon is excellent because many people live a perverse life and have no idea that they are. Perversion is defined as the action of perverting or the condition of being corrupted according to Merriam Webster dictionary. [42] The bible says in Proverb 14:12, "There is a way which seems right unto a man, but the end thereof is the ways of death." Many people today are living their lives unto themselves but are claiming to have a relationship with Jesus.

However, they're in a relationship with the devil. Their minds are distorted into believing what they are doing is right, and God is pleased with them. But I'm here to tell you God is not happy about anyone who worships anything other Him. All forms of perversion are centered around self-gratification. There are three primary ways perversion entraps us: family inheritance, self-created corruption, leadership that operates in depravity.

Regardless of how the perversion was introduced, we have the responsibility to confront and change our behavior to be pleasing unto our savior Jesus Christ. Every individual has the responsibility to learn what perversion they gravitate too and then stay away from that mechanism until wholly delivered. Although even after being delivered, that person may have to refrain from ever coming in contact with that perversion ever in life again by avoiding activities, people, places or things that can cause them to be tempted or fall back into perversion.

CONSEQUENCES

Now that we know what perversion is let's discuss some consequences of it. Those who walk in perversion open the door to the perverse spirit. The perverse sprint brings the following outcomes:

1. Broken Spirit (Proverb 15:4)

The word broke means to be violently separated into parts or SHATTERED according to Merriam Webster.[43] Many of us go through times where people hurt us. If that hurt isn't given unto the Lord, you will be consumed by that hurt causing you to hurt other people or even hurt yourself. Thus, making the way we treat each other very important. Proverbs 18:14 says, "The spirit of a man will sustain his infirmity, but a wounded spirit who can bear?" We have many hurt people giving guidance to others based on their hurt. Have you ever asked a friend for advice about a relationship of the opposite sex? The next thing you know that person compares everything you say about your situation to the hurt they experienced.

Proverb 15:4 says, "A wholesome tongue is a tree of life: but perverseness therein is a breach in the spirit." As people, we must measure everything according to the word of God. If the advice given doesn't line up with the word of God, then you may need to examine the advice giver's life to determine if they were the right person to seek advice from. Ultimately, we should ask the only perfect advice giver who is our God. Therefore, in every situation seek God first, and He will lead you in all truth. Thus, allowing God by the power of deliverance to take your shattered life and make you whole again by submitting your spirit unto Him.

2. Evil Actions (Proverbs 17:20,23)

Evil as a noun means the fact of suffering, misfortune, and wrong doing.[44] The word action mean behavior or conduct according to Merriam Webster.[45] Which means that your behavior or conduct dictates the actions you display. The Bible says in Proverb 17:20,23, "He that hath a froward heart findeth no good: and he that hath a perverse tongue falleth into mischief." Evil action produces evil works. Evil will follow you which will cause chronic worrying (Proverb 19:3), twisting of words (Acts 13:10, 2 Peter 2:14), foolish behavior (Proverbs 1:22, 19:1), contentious behavior (Philippians 2:14-16, 1 Timothy 6:4-5, Titus 3:10-11), filthy mind (Proverb 2:12, 23:33), and abortion (Exodus 20:13, 21:22-25). All of these are evil actions against our King of Kings and Lord of Lord. Remember what John says in Chapter 10 and verse 10 "The thief comes only to steal and kill and destroy: I (Jesus) come that they might have life and that they might have it more abundantly." The devil loves to make rare visits within our lives. However, even after he is gone his presence continues to be felt because of the destruction he leaves behind. Therefore, give no room to the enemy by practicing restraint from sin even when it seems pleasurable.

3. Sexual Perversion (Romans 1:17-32, 2 Timothy 3,2)

Today everything in this world is driven off sexuality. Sexuality turns into sexual gratification which merely is pleasure that turns into a lifetime of lust and destruction. The word sexual is of relating to or associated with sex or the sexes with sexual differentiation or sexual conflict.[46] Many people only talk about the act of sex as being a sin, however, lusting after anything with the intent of self-satisfaction is a sin. Our flesh, eyes or pride draw lust. Sex is a derivative of lust. Lust can come in many forms; sex is just one of the forms. The Bible says that all that is in this world is the lust of the flesh and lust of the eyes and the pride life (1 John 2:16). Lust or desires can destroy us if we don't allow God to lead our path. Without God, our desires become too high and take over our lives and cause us to live unto ourselves, grafting the desires of our own heart which is a major sin. The Bible tells us to delight ourselves in the Lord, and He will give us the desires of our heart (Psalm 37:4). Without the delight in the Lord which brings deliverance and right thinking, we will be forever bound and subject to the lust of this world. Desire usually comes in as a simple pleasure, and before long it consumes us corrupting every aspect of our lives. Therefore, our outcome is death. Thus, we must practice restraint and force every facet of our being to obey Gods word in its entirety.

4. Doctrinal Error (Isaiah 19:14, Romans 1:22-23, 2 Timothy 3:7-8)

Today our churches have become consumed with charismatics, church trending cultural magnetics that no longer hold the standards for holiness and nothing less. Instead, they have become teachers of social norms like the old testament cultures serving anything that gives them pleasure or a feeling of holiness. We know that God is not based on emotions. God's word is based on absolutes because where our Lord is, signs and wonders follow; just as they did when he was on earth many years ago. As the bible states, there is nothing new under the sun. Which means there is nothing further we can come up with in this world because everything has already been done. Therefore, man is continuing the process of not trusting the word of God. The word doctrine means word of God, or something taught or to teach the substance per the Strong Concordance and Bible dictionary.[47]

God's word should be explained with scripture interpreting scripture, context interpreting scripture, and intent interpreting scripture with clear interprets of scripture according to the book foundations of Christian doctrine by Kevin J Conner.[48] Many teachers of the gospel have gone away from biblical truth. Instead, they have corrupted God's word with their belief system. Isaiah 19:14 states, "The LORD hath mingled a perverse spirit in the midst thereof: and they have caused Egypt to err in every work thereof, as a drunken man staggered in his vomit." Church leaders have grieved God, and He has turned them over to the very thing they have practiced. To be more specific, Church leaders have created a drunken people with error. However, our God is going to set the record straight for all who choose not to repent.

5. Atheist (Romans 1:30)

An Atheist is a person who does not believe in the existence of a god or any gods.[49] Atheist have no god. Atheistic allows for self-worship. Even if you have experienced church hurt, there are no excuses for not serving the only true living God. Proverbs 14:2 (NKJV) states, "Those who follow the right path fear the LORD; those who take the wrong path despise him."

Atheism completely separates you for all things that bring life. How many times have you committed an act of sin that was small like a white lie? Before long the white lie turns into lying about anything and everything; even things that are not major within our lives. Therefore, be careful perversion can creep in like a thief in the night but create a presence in your life like the sun on a warm summer's day. The devil is very smart, and he loves to prey on the lost, rejected, wounded and uneducated. These things create avenues for the devil to dwell. Atheist give the devil full rein of their lives because the space that was created for God to live in their life is left empty and dark. Remember, where darkness is the devil will dwell. Therefore, be careful!

ZOLISHA'S TESTIMONY

Now that we have discussed consequences let me tell you my testimony. Perversion made me feel like I was in the will of God; when the reality was, I was far from it. Being raised in another religion caused me to think regardless of what god I served it was my choice of how I wanted to live. That thinking was a lie from the pits of hell. The devil attacked me when I was young. If it hadn't been for believers along my path, I would have been lost forever. Imagine being a person with the wrong concepts of thinking because that way of living has ingrained in you since birth. Imagine only feeling loved when you were dancing provocatively to make the adults around you feel proud. Imagine thinking its normal to be touched by any man inappropriately even if that person is a relative. Imagine these sexual encounters and molestations creating so much devastation in your life you build your own world. This false world then causes you to form a fake life, love, and relationships with nonexistent people.

Before long, I had built a fictional life based on false practices and thinking. Then one day as I was crying out from this very dark place of terror and torture, a voice out of nowhere called out to me asking if I loved them. As soon as I acknowledged that voice, a light came on so bright, I could hardly see anything before me. This light allowed me to see my true reality and the pain was almost too much to bear. But then all at once, I felt a tug of death, anger, hatred, envy, and unforgiveness as another voice reminded me of the circumstances that I was currently experiencing. Then again, a second time I hear that voice again asking me, "Do you love me?" Yet, I hesitated but this time within my hesitation there is even more pain and anguish, but still, I won't open my mouth. But then suddenly with more urgency, I'm asked a third time again by a more robust voice, "Do you love me?" However, this time that darkness I had been living within reminds me of my sins but this time the evil voice names my wrongs off as a judge in a criminal hearing. This evil voice reminds me of my current fornication situation, lying, manipulation, and destructive anger.

The dark evil voice becomes angry and says, "You won't make it because you belong to us." After that voice, everything becomes silent but still. Then out of nowhere, I began to feel the absence of both presences. Suddenly, all at once I felt a slow but steady burning that came from the bottom of my feet all the way up to my head. The burn was internal and hot. So hot I could smell my flesh burning internally. I then opened my eyes and found myself at the altar of a church. I confessed my life unto Jesus Christ. I was introduced to the real supernatural God of Jesus Christ by the fire. This fire was not the baptism of fire but the fire of hell to remind me of where I would spend my time if I didn't surrender my life to God.

GOD'S REDEMPTION

Now let me tell you about the redemptive power of God. God can meet you right where you are just as He did me on that day many years ago. God desires that no man be left to the destruction of this world (1 Timothy 2:4). As you read in my testimony, I was tormented from birth, but God did not leave me there. He knew the time and the place to meet me. We all have a predestined place to be set free by the delivering power of Jesus Christ. Some people's deliverance will come by those who share the gospel or will come by a supernatural visitation of God. Some people will be set free by reading this very testimony. Which one are you? God sent his son so that you may have the opportunity of everlasting life. Jesus told us He didn't come for those who are whole but for those who need a physician (Mark 2:17).

God is not looking for perfection, but someone yielded unto Him. God always gives us a way to get to know Him. However, many of us miss the opportunity because we refuse to admit we need a savior. Don't miss your chance. Take the time to search yourself. No matter if the sin is big or small, God can restore you. All you have to do is acknowledge Him as your God, believe He sent His only begotten Son and confessed your faults to Him. Regardless where you are or what you've been through, God loves you. He knew you before you were ever conceived in your mother's womb. He doesn't care what you've done or who you are. All God wants is a willing vessel who is ready to submit to His will and ways. God loves you, and He is concern about you.

Dear Heavenly Father,

I come to You right now with a bow down head and open heart acknowledging I have fallen short. I need You to make me whole. Father, I recognize that You are the only true living God. Father, I believe You sent your Son to die on the cross for me so that I may have everlasting life. Lord, I confess I'm a sinner, and I'm in need of a Savior. Lord, I need you to make me whole. Father, I ask you to heal all my hurt so that in turn my tongue will be healed so that I will not cause harm to others based on past hurts. Father, I ask you to heal my mind of all wick imagination so that I may be able to take on the mind of Christ. Lord, I ask you to free me from the chains the enemy has me bound by so that I may walk in your teachings and principles. Lord, I give you permission to rest, rule, and abide in my life. Lord, I ask for You to make me more sensitive to you. Open my mind to Your teachings and my ears to Your voice. Lord, help me to find a church home where I can grow and walk in the calling in which You have for me. Lord, I thank You for Your saving grace. I thank you, Lord, for not leaving me on the path I was on. Father, I ask all these things in your son Jesus' name. Amen.

CHAPTER TWENTY
Pride

BY ALEX HARDING

Pride is a root cause that makes people think irrationally throughout their lifetime in the decision-making process. According to Merriam Webster's Dictionary, pride can be defined as the quality or state of being proud.[50] Proverbs 16:18 (NKJV) says, "Pride goes before destruction and a haughty spirit before a fall." I've seen this problem reoccur in my life for as long as I can remember. I lost plenty of opportunities, experiences, and numerous failed relationships. Pride cost me everything. Since we have the foundation laid out and a sense of what pride is about, let's go another route. Let's zoom in on the consequences of this pride monster.

CONSEQUENCES

1. Envy

1 Corinthians 13:4 (NKJV) says "Love suffers long and is kind, Love does not Envy, Love does not parade itself is not puffed up." You can't just be walking around all puffed up; chest

all puffed up like you're God's greatest creation. You must humble yourself. If not, others will do it for you. You will have jealousy, and that's both genders disliking you at some point. You have no one to blame but yourself because this is all from your actions. Like my father would always tell me, "Look in the mirror. You are your own worst enemy."

2. Destruction

Proverbs 16:18 (NKJV) says "Pride goes before destruction, and a haughty spirit before a fall." Your pride will destroy many areas in your life: loss of jobs, wages, properties, and family. It will seem as if your whole life was destroyed. When you are prideful people are going to be aiming and shooting to destroy you intentionally from past hurt. Yes! Your pride from last week or last year will be in remembrance and try to hinder and ruin your future. The only person that can restore you is God. Everything will be out of your control. Honestly, by this time, you'll need Him, and the good news is He'll always be there! Unlike us, God never changes.

3. Shame

Proverbs 11:2 says, "When pride cometh, then cometh shame but with the lowly is wisdom." Shame is one of the worst feelings for a prideful person. When it's all said and done this is exactly how you're going to feel. All the times you just knew you were right and then to find out you're wrong will leave you feeling shameful. Pride also results in taking others for granted until they leave or abandoned you. Trust me inside your going to face shame. You may have so much pride that you refuse to admit to yourself your shame. When pride operates that heavily in your life, you can't even be real with yourself. At the end of the day, you'll be the one hurting.

4. Deposed

Daniel 5:20 (NKJV) says, "But when his heart was lifted up and his spirit was hardened in pride, he was deposed from his kingly throne, and they took his glory from him." Do you think someone wants to listen to a boastful, prideful, arrogant person? Some may feel as if you're unworthy and don't deserve it. Typically, when that happens, that's when the confiscations and possibly confrontations will arise. Everything that took your hard work, time, energy, and efforts to accomplish is gone just like that. Don't think for a second that the same people you were walking over will have mercy or sympathy for you. I learned that's when you genuinely feel payback when you're at your lowest, weakest, most vulnerable moments.

ALEX'S TESTIMONY

For me, it all started when I was younger. Although my parents weren't together, they loved me a lot. They both were hard workers and worked throughout my life at their same jobs over 25 years. They were big on grades. Good grades got me good rewards, so I excelled. I was talented in baseball and music. In Junior High School, I was elected most talented and well-dressed. I believe that's where the pride stemmed from. By my senior year, I had a nice car with some nice rims and neighborhood notoriety with music. I was opening concerts with major artists, and meeting girls wasn't hard for me after a while. The thing that was hardest for me was swallowing my pride and excepting when things didn't go my way. I would disconnect with any and everybody who wouldn't live up to my expectations. Some of them were good people. Some of them genuinely showed real love. I was so blinded by my ego and having my way. I was willing to lose to replace them. I was walking around with so many chips on my shoulder from past hurt: failed relationships, unfaithful girlfriends, and the what 'ifs' about how things would have been if my parents would have stayed together. You know the usual teenage mind.

By graduation, I started working and still make songs for my friends. I connected with a popular producer and remembered praying to God for help and clarity with this song. The song was a financial investment entirely out of my normal. By the next two to four years, the song went from a neighborhood favorite to statewide success. It was an instant classic in the state of Louisiana. I don't think anything can take over a young man's mind more than having the desires of his heart right before his eyes: beautiful women, popularity, not to mention getting paid for doing what you love doing. So, you can imagine my arrogance level was all over the place. Anyone who doubted me in the past, I flaunted my success in their face. Some would say I was stuck up and thought I was all that. I was doing a lot, and it brought a lot of hate. I had so much pride that I would hate you back.

My mother would be so worried and prayed so many prayers for and over me. She was always into church, taught the youth religion, and sang in the choir throughout my life. She was very proud of me as an artist but so worried about me as her son. I was moving so fast. Proverbs 18:7 says, "A fool's mouth is his destruction, and his lips are the snare of his soul." I started having trouble with law enforcement, difficulty with jobs, and problems in relationships. I was wrecking all my cars and even was having trouble now with my parents. My pride was starting to bring me down. I was on probation from 18 to 26 years old. A lot of things that I wanted to do, I couldn't. Some opportunities also closed by this time. I had burned a lot of bridges. I didn't want to get stuck where I was ending up. God would always get me on my face and bring me right back to Him. I had to cry, pray, and seek Him to reverse this curse of pride because it was hindering me.

GOD'S REDEMPTION

Proverbs 19:4 says, "Wealth maketh many friends but the poor is separated from his neighbor." I have been in this position also from the effects of my pride after losing almost everything, or at least, that's what I thought, or at least that's what it felt like. The numbers that used to call wasn't calling anymore. Better yet, the numbers I used to call weren't answering. Being broke is like an infection, nobody wants to encounter you. You're bad luck to superstitious people. But in all those times when I had nobody to call, I just started calling and relying on God. Reading about His love, compassion, promises, help, and deliverance, I needed all of that! Psalm 107:20 says, "He sent his word, and healed them, and delivered them from their destructions." I brought study bibles to understand His words better. First, it started with just reading. Reading manifested to applying. Applying led to the urge to serve. He knows how to get our attention to get the glory. It's a process, but along the way, I'm learning it's well worth it. I'm still praying, fasting and asking for help to get a pure heart because battling my tongue is a daily battle. I know that's the first step is admitting where the problem starts and allowing the Holy Spirit to purge away pride and its symptoms. Sinfulness, resentment, jealousy, or hate that I may have still inside of me will break free, released, and cast out into the swine. Overcome this obstacle. Climb this mountain and when you get up, never forget how you got there.

Dear Heavenly Father,

Lord, I bless your name. Lord, I magnify you. Lord, I need you. Please overtake this possession of pride that's trying to control my life, mind, and feelings when my ego sends me mixed signals. Lord, Ephesians 4:22-24 (NKJV) says "That you put off concerning your former conduct the old man which grows corrupt according to the deceitful lusts and be renewed in the spirit of your mind. And that you put on a new man which was created according to God in true righteousness and holiness". Lord, I plead the blood of Jesus over my feelings and reactions. Lord, I plead the blood of Jesus over my mind. No weapon formed against me shall prosper and any fiery darts of the enemy will be shut down in the name of Jesus. Isaiah 14:14-15 (NKJV) says, "I will ascend above the heights of the clouds I will be like the Most High. Yet you shall be brought down to Sheol to the lowest depths of the pit." I decree and declare nothing that the enemy tries to work me up with will work. I decree and declare that Lord, you are my strength and my shield, and nothing is out of your control. Take any pride, resentment, hatred, and jealousy out of my soul. Refill and refine within me a pure heart. I ask all of this in Jesus mighty matchless name. Amen.

CHAPTER TWENTY ONE
Prostitution

BY KIMBERLY MOSES

Many people around the world are paying for sex. Some countries sell underage children to wealthy business men. These girls are kidnapped, shipped overseas, drugged and forced to work as sex slaves in brothels. These girls are pimped out and afraid to run away to get help. Some women are selling their bodies to pay their bills or to make fast cash. Prostitution can even be traced in the Bible. There were many temple prostitutes (1 Kings 14:24). Prostitution is to offer indiscriminately for sexual intercourse, especially for money.[51] Deuteronomy 23:17 (CEB) says, "People of Israel, don't any of you ever be temple prostitutes." Prostitution can cost you everything! Now that you know what prostitution is let's discuss the consequences.

CONSEQUENCES

1. Ungodly Soul Ties

People who are prostitutes have ungodly soul ties with the people they have intercourse with. A soul tie is like a linkage in the soul realm between two people.[52] They might get attached to someone emotionally and physically. Whatever spirits that person has will transfer to you. For instance, if the person you slept with has the spirit of fear than it will transfer to you. Before you know it, you will start having anxiety attacks.

2. Sickness

Prostitution can lead to all kind of sexual diseases. Sexual transmitted diseases include crabs, gonorrhea, chlamydia, syphilis, HIV, herpes, warts, and the list continues. There is a high chance of getting re-infected again once they received treatment. Latex doesn't protect against all diseases especially if the condom has been tampered with.

3. Jail

There is punishment in certain states for prostitution. The punish varies from state to state or country to country. Some penalties include fines, prison, or death. Even if someone is involved by transporting a prostitute or pimping them, they will be punished as well. There are many undercover police officers on the streets cracking down on prostitution. Now that we have covered some of the consequences of prostitution let's see how it can cost you everything!

JALISA'S TESTIMONY

Jalisa had goals of being a video vixen. All she cared about were her looks and her body. She would work out to sculpt her body to draw more attention to herself. She loved fashion and money. She didn't have a regular job. Her job was sleeping with men for money. The men she slept with had different social statuses. Some were crooked attorneys, corrupt police officers, drug dealers, and some were married. She knew what to tell these men to have them spend most of their paychecks on her. She enjoyed travel, shopping, and eating fancy foods. She especially enjoyed partying. Everything to Jalisa was fun and games. She was always very careful but soon her world would come crashing down.

Jalisa met a new man in his hotel room. His name was Corey. Corey was older and seemed well established in life. What Jalisa didn't know was that Corey was HIV positive. He was on a rampage of infecting different women with HIV because he was upset that he got infected. He would meet different women online or in person and convince them to have sex with him. Corey would bring the condoms. He would stick several needles through the package. When he would sleep with these women, he made sure the lights were dim or even dark so they wouldn't notice. Since the condom already had several holes in it, the condom always ripped during penetration.

When the intercourse was over, the women noticed how the condom ripped. This is how Jalisa got infected with HIV. She was a victim of Corey's scheme. After the act was finish, he paid her fee and left. Jalisa shook off the dirty feeling when she thought about the torn condemn. She continued to live a fast life. A week later, she was watching the news and saw Corey. He had been arrested for infecting over 75 women with HIV. Immediately her heart dropped. She went to the local clinic and found out that she was HIV positive. She contacted the health department to report Corey, and she discovered that there was a class action suit against him.

GOD'S REDEMPTION

All Jalisa could think about was being sick and dying. She was scared, and she didn't know what to do. She didn't even want to prostitute anymore. She had panic attacks almost daily. Nothing was coping her pain. One day she was watching YouTube. She wanted to research people who were also HIV positive. As she was watching video after video, something caught her eye. She saw a video titled, "Healed of Aids." She thought the video was click bait. "No way," she told herself. She couldn't resist so she clicked and watched it. She saw a preacher praying for people who said that they were sick. She saw people falling out and speaking in a weird language. She didn't understand that they were speaking in tongues.

She watched people testified how the doctors couldn't find any trace of HIV in their blood. Jalisa was desperate, so she started following the preacher in the video. She looked him up on the internet. She found out that he was always traveling to different cities. His next event was two hours away. Jalisa decided that she would go to this because she wanted to be healed like the people in the video. A month passed, and Jalisa was sick from taking the prescribed medicines. She pushed past how she felt and went to the event.

When she got to the event, it was packed. There was standing room only, so she found a seat in the back of the room. She began to feel something that she never felt in her life. She felt the presence of God. She started to shake and cry during the worship. Everything that was spoken hit her heart. She felt like she was the only one in the room. The minister started praying for the sick after he finished his sermon. When he called out HIV, Jalisa got hot all over. She was feeling the fire of God. She knew something was happening but didn't quite understand. She felt intense heat. She started wailing and shaking all over. It looked like she was having a seizure. She tried to stand up but collapsed on the floor. She ended up being on the floor for about 30 minutes. One of the ushers placed a blanket upon her and helped her get up when she came out of the glory.

The minister called people to the altar to receive salvation. Jalisa ran to the front. She accepted Jesus into her heart and later testified that she was healed. After the service, she drove for 2 hours back home. She knew that God healed her. She requested blood work the next day. When the results came back, the lab couldn't find any trace of HIV in her blood. Jalisa was so happy that she sent a copy of her blood work to the minister. She couldn't stop praising God. She knew that He orchestrated her steps to the YouTube video that day. He healed her. She turned her back on her old life style and embraced her new life instead.

She wanted everyone to know about the miracle. She testified on local radio. Doors opened for her to go on TV. She told her story in different churches. God opened many doors for her to travel across the nation empowering women to live holy as she shares her story. You may be in prostitution, but you are worth so much more. There is a new life today that you can have in Jesus. Are you ready to accept this new life?

Dear Heavenly Father,

I humble myself and repent. I don't want to sell my body for sex anymore. It's degrading, and I feel so disgusting afterward. Lord, deliver me from prostitution. Bless me with finances and the wisdom on how to be a good steward of it. Lord, give me strength so I can do the right thing in life. Draw me closer to you. Father do a work in me. Protect me. Thank you for answering this prayer in Jesus' name. Amen.

CHAPTER TWENTY TWO
Rape

BY ALEXANDER YOUNG

We all have heard the horror stories about rape and the destructive force and impact it has on communities, families, relationships, and the individual. According to Merriam Webster, rape is defined as unlawful sexual activity and usually sexual intercourse carried out forcibly or under threat of injury against a person's will or with a person who is incapable of valid consent because of mental illness, mental deficiency, intoxication, unconsciousness, or deception.[53] In the book of 2 Samuel 13:1-34 it shows how a family is torn apart by rape when Amnon violated Absalom's sister Tamar because he was in love with her. Amnon received deceptive advice on how to get her by his friend Jonadab. Rape is common among young girls and women. However, it is rare that you hear about teenage boys being raped by other boys. By the end of this chapter, you will understand how being on the other side of the offense of rape cost me everything.

CONSEQUENCES

Rape has damaging effects and has a wide range of consequences. Of course, there are the consequences the offender must face, but let's look at the other side of the offense to see what implications the victim is suffering.

1. Physical Damage:

Rape victims have physical damage which is any abnormalities to the body that may cause specific function impairment. Impairments are bruising, soreness, bleeding (anal), or difficulty walking.

2. Psychological disorder:

According to Merriam Webster, a psychological disorder is an impairment of the mind and emotions or disorganization of personality.[54] A person's state of mind will not be the same after a traumatizing event like when rape occurs. Not knowing how to respond afterward was one of my mental breakdowns. Too often many people have judged others on how they act. They judged them without knowing if they are going or have been through something.

3. Aloofness:

Aloofness is a state to which a person distances themselves from the population and even friends and family.[55] In a sense, a person doesn't feel alone but wants to be left alone. I interacted with the crowd, but at the same time I didn't talk or smile as much as I used to around others.

4. Mistrust:

Rape is common amongst friends and family. It can cause one to have a state of mind that no one is trustworthy to be around because of fear or harm. This mindset can be long term or short term. It's hard to trust again after being hurt. Believe me, it's hard. The term, "Keep your friends close, but your enemies closer," gives you an idea on the mistrust spectrum in depth.

These are a few consequences. Though it might seem as if these are side effects, it was my overall behavior of how I functioned to live with what happened. I lost friends. I hid in anger. I gave up my character. I lived as if nothing happened. But now let me tell you my story about how rape cost me everything.

ALEXANDER'S TESTIMONY

I remember like it was yesterday. I was a teenager in high school, the underdog of the crowd, but mainly focused on being a good student. I had friends and acquaintances, but I sometimes was bullied by some of the students. I was not a popular guy like my friends were. I still remember that some people close to me said, "You're too gullible and too nice. That's why people take advantage of you." So, what happened? It was after school, I went home, and did my homework. I relaxed a bit. Two hours later, three of my friends came over, and I invited them in. We talked, listened to music, and played video games. Then one of them snuck up from behind and hit me in the back of my head with a bottle. I was knocked down, and that's when the horror began.

The other two guys rushed in. They grabbed and seized me. As I fought and struggled to get free, one of them took a bottle and cracked it on my left jaw. Another person punched me in my right jaw. I was over powered and overwhelmed. I was in a powerless state, barely conscious, and could hardly see what was going on. I felt my pants coming down, and the guy in the back begin to penetrate my rear while the other two held me. I was crying and still trying to fight, but one of the guys holding my arms punched me in my eye. Then the other began to penetrate orally. I'm still struggling and hurting at the same time because I was still being rear-ended. The guys proceeded to hold my mouth open and was successful. They each took turns and reached the point of climax regardless of me fighting.

After they finished, one of them took a bottle and knocked me out. They left the house. I woke up in a state of shock and fear because I couldn't believe that these guys whom I called friends since the 7th grade would do such an act. My mother was in a state of panic because she saw all the bruises on me. She wondered what happened. I hid the truth from her and lied. "I got into a fight after school," I said. I thought it was over, but it wasn't. Rumors went around the school saying that I was a homosexual, and I liked doing things with guys. The guys who raped me said that I tried to come on to them.

Students began to look at me differently and did not talk to me. Some of my real friends wanted to help and console me because they didn't believe the rumors. But I pushed them all away. I was in a state of mind that I couldn't trust anyone. That deep-seated mistrust was built up anger. As time went on, I began to live as if nothing ever happened. I was slowly interacting with the crowd that still connected with me. But truthfully, I was scared to talk to anyone from that point on. The happiness that I showed was nothing but a phony mask to cover up my real issue and feelings.

GOD'S REDEMPTION

For years I lived in silence on that subject. After four years in ministry and drawing even more closer to God, I found myself opening up to Him. I shared that hidden secret that was causing internal bleeding mentally and spiritually. I found it easier to let it go after talking with my significant other and my spiritual sister about what happened. During those conversations, God revealed to me that I didn't change whom I am. Most men would say that they lost their manhood which is not the case. I maintained my manhood. I didn't allow what happened to me dictate my sexual preference. In other words, I didn't make my situation an excuse to do something I'm not supposed to or be something that I am not. God redeemed me from an internal wound in my heart. He delivered me of the fear of how people would look at me if I told them what I experienced.

Dear Heavenly Father,

I come humbly before You to thank You for who You are. You have kept me all these years and chosen me to be a mouth piece for Your kingdom. I pray that someone will be delivered and healed from any deep-seated pain within their heart. Lord, heal every victim of rape in Jesus' name. Lord, I love you and thank You in Jesus' name. Amen.

CHAPTER TWENTY THREE

BY KIMBERLY MOSES

Have you ever wanted to make someone pay for the hurt they caused you? I surely did. I wanted revenge. I wanted the person who hurt me to suffer the way that I was experiencing. If you ever wanted revenge, then you probably felt the same way. According to Merriam-Webster, revenge can be defined as to avenge (oneself or another) usually by retaliating in kind or degree; to inflict injury in return for or a desire for vengeance or retribution.[56] When you want revenge, you will do whatever you have to do to see it happen. Revenge isn't pleasing in the sight of God. Romans 12:19 says, "Dearly beloved, avenge not yourselves, but rather give place unto wrath: for it is written, Vengeance is mine; I will repay, saith the Lord." When we surrender our will of taking matters into our own hands and give it to the Lord, He will avenge us. If we don't trust the Lord to avenge us and seek revenge, it will cost us everything! Now that we know what revenge is let's discuss its consequences.

CONSEQUENCES

1. Jail

When your heart is full of revenge, you are blinded and can't see the consequences. You aren't concerned with being arrested for your actions. When you take matters into your own hands, you aren't trusting God to fight for you. When you take the law in your own hands, the police can't do their jobs. Romans 13:1 says, "Let every soul be subject unto the higher powers. For there is no power but of God: the powers that be are ordained of God." People go to jail all the time as a result of revenge. Maybe they were fired and mistreated at their job. If the person takes revenge, they might shoot up their old workplace. Retaliation will result in jail time especially if lives are lost and destroyed.

2. Bitter

Bitterness consumes your heart when you are full of revenge. It's almost as if you can taste or see the blood of your enemy. You want the person that hurt you to pay the price. When you are bitter, you have a hard time forgiving the person who offended you. When you walk in bitterness, there is no peace within. Bitterness will defile you and cause you to be a vessel for the devil to use. Nothing good comes out of it. The Bible warns us that the 'root of bitterness' will cause trouble. It leads to a vindictive spirit. Hebrews 12:15 says, "Looking diligently lest any man fail of the grace of God; lest any root of bitterness springing up trouble you, and thereby many be defiled;"

3. Time

Being revengeful is time consuming. It's all you think about. You go to bed thinking about how you can get even. You wake up thinking of more ways to bring your plan to pass. Not only are you wasting your time but energy. It takes energy to stalk a person to find out their next moves to execute a plan of revenge. It takes resources such as money to get weapons, spy gear, etc. You can channel that negative energy into positive energy by working on your calling in life. Psalm 90:12 says, "So teach us to number our days, that we may apply our hearts unto wisdom." Now that we discussed some consequences let me tell you how revenge cost me everything!

KIMBERLY'S TESTIMONY

In 2013, I was backslidden and lukewarm. The peace of God that I once had left my life. I was dealing with anxiety and going through marital problems. I wanted to live right, so I prayed. I prayed a very simple prayer that would change my life. "Lord, I repent of everything. I want to be close to you." I had no idea that I was entering a wilderness season and would lose everything. As a result of this prayer, I got very close to God. Closer than I could ever imagine. In the summer of 2013, my ex-husband told me that his job was relocating to Colorado. He asked me to go with him so that we could work on our marriage. We were previously separated, and now we were reconciling. He promised a fresh start for us. I agreed to go with him. I decided to not go to any medical schools on the east coast but try schools in the mid-west. I gave up the opportunity of pursuing enrollment to these potential schools to follow my husband at the time.

When we arrived in Colorado, things were okay between us for a while then things headed south. One day, my ex-husband was playing basketball and tore his Achilles tendon. He had to get surgery. I took care of him and nursed him back to health. I noticed a change in his behavior. There was an invisible wall between us. He wasn't communicating or affectionate. He changed his passwords on his phone and computer. He started coming home later than usual. I knew something wasn't right, so I did some investigating.

After many attempts, I was able to figure out his new passwords. I discovered that he opened a new email account and was communicating with one of his ex-girlfriends. They were sending each other inappropriate photos. I knew who this woman was because I met her and her husband before. Her name was Melody. Out of pain and rage, I looked up her husband online and got his information. I then forwarded him all the emails that I saw. I confronted my ex-husband about it, and he lied about everything. A couple of hours later, Melody called my ex-husband. I was so upset and felt so disrespected. I cursed her out for calling my husband. Melody's husband got on the phone and cursed out my ex-husband.

A few days passed, I thought that my ex-husband would be faithful, but I was wrong. I discovered that he and Melody were secretly still planning to meet. I found airline tickets to the city where she lived. Once again out of rage, I called the airline pretending to be my ex-husband and canceled the tickets. When he found out what I did, he was furious and left the house for a few days. He wouldn't answer any of my calls. I was so hurt. I didn't know where he was or if he had seen Melody. As an act of desperation, I checked into a hotel because I wanted to be gone just in case he came home. I thought that if he came back to an empty house, he would start to treat me better. I was disappointed because it didn't work.

I decided that I was wasting money after staying in a hotel for a couple of nights. I didn't know when he would return, so I came home. When he came back home a few days later, he was unapologetic. I threaten to leave him, but he didn't even care. He had hatred towards me. He started to abuse me verbally by calling me names, belittling my character, and throwing my past in my face. I was severely depressed. My house was no longer peaceful but chaotic. I slept in the bedroom, and he slept on the couch. This was not what my ex-husband promised me. He brought me out to Colorado to work on our marriage, but all we were doing was fighting.

I decided to get help. I began getting counseling at the church that I was attending. My ex-husband refused to go with me, so I went alone. The advice helped initially, but I needed more help. Also, I decided to see another counselor who wasn't spiritual because I thought it would give me a better outlook on things. For months, I went to counseling and learned many helpful things I could do to better myself.

I began to pray and seek God. I started reading the bible more often, but I was far from where I needed to be in God. I was tired of being in a bad marriage, so I took matters into my own hands. I put all my ex-husbands' electronics in my car and wrote him a note. "You will never see your electronics again unless you straighten up." I wrote the letter and then headed to church. In the middle of the church, I heard the voice of the enemy. I could easily hear him because he was speaking to me daily while I was dealing with anxiety. He was telling me that I was going to die and to kill myself. For some odd reason, I listened to him that day. The devil told me to go outside and leave the church service.

I got up in the middle of the church service and walked outside. When I stepped outside, I saw my ex-husband driving off. I knew he had gotten his electronics back. He went in my car and took them. Immediately, I blacked out. Rage began to roar inside me, and revenge overtook me. I lost control and reacted underneath demonic influence. I jumped in my car, chased my ex-husband, and rammed my car into his. At that moment, I felt hate. I hated him for everything he put me through. After, I hit his car I snapped back into reality. I was scared and fled from the accident.

I went back home and started to pack bags to head out of state. The police were looking for me, and they quickly caught up with me. They arrested me. This night was the started of me losing everything. When I was in jail, I was dealing with the spirit of murder. I was plotting ways to kill my ex-husband. When it was time to stand before the judge to find out what my set bail would be to be released, I was served divorce papers.

When I got out of jail, I couldn't return to my house because of a restraining order that was in effect. I only had $65 in my account, and I got a hotel room. I called my family from out of state. They came to help me find a place to stay. For the first time in my life, I was no longer in control. I lost everything!

GOD'S REDEMPTION

One of the consequences of my behavior was two years of probation. I remember crying about this. I wanted to get as far as I could from Colorado. I wanted to start over in life in my home town in North Carolina. The trial was real no matter how much I wanted to run. I couldn't believe I was so foolish. I was stuck in the state of Colorado, and I had to do time. I was upset, and I still wanted revenge on my ex-husband. However, as the trial intensified, I had to repent and allow God to change me sincerely. I hated my ex-husband. I wanted him to die.

I started attending church again every time the doors opened. As I sat in these services, the word of God would penetrate my heart. My eyes opened, and I saw how destructive I was. I prayed that God would change me. God told me to pray for my ex-husband, this was the last thing that I wanted to do. I was so angry at him. I knew in my heart to please God that I had to pray. When I first started praying for my ex-husband, the prayers were short. As the weeks passed, the prayers got longer. Sometimes, I would pray for him for hours. It seemed like things got worse in the beginning, but I began to see God's restoration. He was molding me in the process. I let go of all control and allowed God to be in control. I stopped reacting in anger and learned how to bite my tongue. I learned to walk away from confrontation.

Months went by, and I didn't hear from my ex-husband, but one day he called me and apologized for everything. I apologized as well, and I truly meant it. I didn't want him to die anymore. I wanted him to be okay and to be happy. I realized that God took the hate out of my heart and placed His love in my heart. Now my ex-husband and I no longer argue. We get along, and God gets all the Glory! Revenge cost me everything. It's not worth losing everything. Let it go because you don't want to make a decision that you will regret one day.

Dear Heavenly Father,

I confess that I am full of revenge. I am angry, and I want justice. Help me to let it go. Bless me not to take matters into my own hands. Lord, deliver me from the spirit of revenge. I yield my thoughts to you. I cast out the spirit of revenge from my mind and heart today. I want to be free. I'm tired of holding onto grudges and walking in un-forgiveness. I forgive the person that has hurt me. I bless them. Lord, keep me and prevent me being revengeful. Thank you for answering this prayer in Jesus' name. Amen.

CHAPTER TWENTY FOUR
Slothfulness

BY KIMBERLY MOSES

Often in life we have lazy days and don't feel like going to work, doing housework, or run errands. Might've just wanted to lie around all day, eat a hearty meal, and sleep most of the day away. However, we must push past this feeling so we can accomplish specific tasks, not get in trouble, or worst. What happens if someone doesn't overcome this feeling on a regular basis? This person is considered slothful. According to Merriam Webster, the word sloth is a disinclination to action or labor: indolence or spiritual apathy and inactivity.[57] Many people miss out on opportunities and blessings due to being slothful. Proverbs 19:15 says, "Slothfulness casteth into a deep sleep; and an idle soul shall suffer hunger." You can't prosper being lazy. Slothfulness can cost you everything! Now that we have defined slothfulness let's look at its consequences.

CONSEQUENCES

1. Poor Performance

Slothfulness can cause poor performance in many areas such as school and work. For instance, a student is lazy and doesn't put the necessary study time in to pass their tests or the course. They will end up failing the grade level or class because they aren't performing well. Another example is a worker being lazy on their job. They will start taking shortcuts to finish faster that can result in hazards or death depending on their line of work. Their overall work performance will be low which will result in termination. A lazy person will have a difficult time keeping a job.

2. Bad Health

Lazy people probably won't be the healthiest people. Instead of exercising they will eat and lay around. Over time, they might start gaining weight that results in various diseases such as hypertension, joint pain, diabetes, heart disease and more. A lazy person's hygiene probably won't be the best. They might go days without showering, brushing their teeth, or doing their hair. Also, their appearance might not even be the best. They might have wrinkles in their clothes because they are too lazy to iron them.

3. Poverty

A lazy person will live a life of poverty because they aren't willing to put forth the effort it takes to advance. As mentioned earlier, they will have a difficult time keeping employment and will struggle. Proverbs 10:4 says, "He becometh poor that dealeth with a slack hand: but the hand of the diligent maketh rich." In other words, a person becomes poor because of a slack hand or laziness. A person becomes rich due to hard work. If you work hard now, you can enjoy the results of the provision later. Your investment will pay off if you put in the work. Now that we have covered some consequences of laziness let's look at how slothfulness can cost you everything.

BRUCE'S TESTIMONY

Bruce was a handsome man with a lot of potential, but he refused to apply himself. He only graduated high school because his parents forced him to complete it. He almost didn't graduate because he overslept and was tardy all the time. After he barely graduated, he refused to go to college to gain a skill set. He faced a lot of tension with his parents because they were pressuring him to do something with his life. Bruce didn't listen. He just wanted to sit around and eat pizza or Chinese food and watch television. To keep peace where he lived, he got a pizza delivery job.

On his job, he met a lot of college students who were preparing for their future. Years went by, and Bruce still worked the same pizza delivery job. He stayed there because he got discounts on pizza and he would often get free pizzas that were left over at the end of the night. Bruce saw people come and go from the pizzeria that worked with him. One day an old employee name Shawn came to order a large pepperoni pizza. He looked great.

He was wearing an expensive suit and watch. He was a CEO of a pharmaceutical company. Shawn remembered Bruce and told him about a fantastic opportunity that could bring in millions.

Bruce denied the opportunity. A couple of years went by, and Bruce was in his early thirties. He picked up the newspaper one day and seen Shawn on the front page. There was a headline story about how his company was doing great and helping many people in the community. Bruce was glad to see his old friend doing well, but he started to regret the day when he turned down the opportunity. He knew that if he would've said yes to Shawn many years ago, he would've been well off. However, he still depended on his parents to take care of him. Bruce was still living in his parents home due to his laziness.

Things were about to get worst for Bruce. One night, the pizzeria was vandalized and burnt to the ground. This pizzeria was a family business, and there weren't any franchises of it. He didn't know what to do anymore because he was without a job. He had a hard time gaining employment due to his minimum education level. His parents were tired of him making excuses. He started to feel depressed and began to drink alcohol to cope with his pain. He told himself that he would never be anything in life.

GOD'S REDEMPTION

One day Bruce was up late at night and flipping through the channels. He was bored and couldn't find anything to watch. He turned past the gospel channel and stopped because he saw a lady that looked crazy to him. He paused to mocked her because of her message. She was talking about how ants are hard workers, and we need to be like them. He wanted to turn the channel, but his eyes were glued to the television. The preacher's words started to penetrate his heart. He began to feel the presence of God in His room. He didn't know what it was at the time, but all he could do was cry.

He realized how his laziness affected him and regretted wasting years of his life doing nothing. He was in his thirties, living with his parents, no wife, and no children. He wanted his life to mean something. He wanted to do something of purpose in life. Bruce began to watch different ministers on the gospel network, and he was led into the sinner's prayer. He prayed to get to know Jesus and to get his life together so he could move out of his parent's home and have his own family.

Bruce didn't know any local churches in his area, so he connected with the minister on television that fed his spirit the most. He repented for being lazy and went to college. In college, he got a degree in business. While he was in school, he was able to get a job as a stocker overnight in a grocery store. He started to save money and didn't waste money anymore on food and games. He began to listen to sermons online to encourage himself and read his bible daily. He was able to get a small business loan after he finished school. Bruce stepped out in faith and found a building. He renovated it and turned it into a pizzeria which was on the news for having great tasting pizza.

Bruce had learned the art of making pizza because he worked at a pizzeria for years before it burned down. Bruce was a natural. He was able to move out of his parents' home and get established on his own. One of the regular customers got a job there. Her name was Michelle. Bruce and Michelle eventually started dating and shortly after they got married and had a baby. They were happy. Bruce's parents were happy as well. Bruce donates pizza to churches or different events from time to time because He knows that the Lord broke slothfulness off his life. His life is now a life of purpose. He blesses the community with his delicious pizza, and his business is prospering today.

You may be lazy, but the power of God can break it off you. You may have missed out on some great opportunities, but God is a God of multiple chances. Will you pray with me today?

Dear Heavenly Father,

I confess my sin of being lazy. I repent. I want to do better in life. I yield my mind and heart to Jesus today. Set me free Lord and deliver me. I decree that I will be a hard worker. I renounce slothfulness and all its negative consequences. I decree over my life that I will be like the ant and not be sluggish. I will be wise and study the ways of the ant. I decree that I can do all things through Christ that strengths me. I decree that God is on my side and I will make it in Jesus' name. Amen.

CHAPTER TWENTY FIVE

BY KIMBERLY MOSES

People steal all the time. They take other people's ideas and work by plagiarism. They steal someone's identity and ruin their credit. They steal money, jewelry, clothes, cars, and more. Some people even steal opportunities because they were plotting to get it from the start. Stealing is taking the property of another wrongfully and especially as a habitual or regular practice.[58] Stealing is what the devil does best because he comes to kill, steal, and destroy everything in his path (John 10:10). Exodus 20:15 says, "Thou shalt not steal." Stealing can cost you everything. Now that we have discussed what stealing is let's consider the consequences.

CONSEQUENCES

1. Jail

Charges vary depending on the amount or value of the item that was stolen. For instance, some people may be placed on probation or must pay a fine for the number of items stolen. Some people must pay back restitution. Some people may be sentenced several years in prison. Charges also vary if someone is considered a juvenile, first time offender, or repeat offender. Laws vary upon jurisdictions, but there are consequences for theft.

2. No Salvation

God loves the sinner but hates the sin. One day everyone will be judged. On judgment day, a theft will see all the times they stole and sentenced to an eternity in hell. Thieves have wickedness in their hearts that they refused to deal with. God looks at our hearts (1 Samuel 16:7). 1 Corinthians 6:9-10 says, "Know ye not that the unrighteous shall not inherit the kingdom of God? Be not deceived: neither fornicators, nor idolaters, nor adulterers, nor effeminate, nor abusers of themselves with mankind, Nor thieves, nor covetous, nor drunkards, nor revilers, nor extortioners, shall inherit the kingdom of God."

3. Loss of Rights

Imagine being banned from places and having your face put up on a board for all the employees and customers to see. You might be humiliated. Many thieves are banned from restaurants, grocery stores, convenient stores, outlets, and retail stores. Their name, number, and address are on a black list which means employees aren't to do business with them. In some states, thieves can't have firearms.

Now that we know what the consequences are for stealing let's see how it can cost you everything.

LUCY'S TESTIMONY

Lucy always enjoyed living life on the wild side. She enjoyed the thrill of getting away with things. She always broke the laws. She was a cheat, and always found ways to get over on people. She grew up poor and hung around older kids on her block. She saw them steal food from a convenient store and get away with it. So, she started stealing too at ten years of age. Each time, she became craftier. She would steal jewelry from different department stores. She stole makeup, clothing, and electronics. Each time, she got more creative. She would have people that she trained to come along to cause a distraction such as a fight. When the person behind the counter went to help break up the argument, she would take money out of the register or leave with the product out of the store.

Lucy had so much merchandise. She thought that she was the best at her trade and wanted to see how far she could go without being caught. One day as she was driving, she passed some big beautiful homes. "That's it," she thought to herself. I will start robbing houses. Lucy had all the necessary spy wear so she would have no difficulty breaking into a safe. Lucy began to target homes and their residents. She knew their schedule and researched the layout of the home. When the family would be away, she would make her move. She would enter the house and take things of value such as jewelry, money, etc. She was in and out in five minutes before the authorities arrived.

Lucy continued to steal from homes, and the local news station was on alert. They warned all residents in the area to step up their security systems. One day, Lucy broke into the wrong house. She had targeted a home, but she miscounted the number of people who lived there. She didn't know that there was an elderly man that barely left the house. One day the elderly man was in his chair watching television, and he heard the alarm in the house go off. He immediately got his gun in his closet. After he grabbed the gun, he came face to face with Lucy. He began to shoot, and Lucy ran, but one of the bullets hit her spine. When the bullet hit her spine, it shattered in several places. Lucy dropped to the floor and when the policed arrived an ambulance was called.

Lucy was taken to the emergency room then to the operating room. They had to stop the bleeding and repair her spinal column. A steel rod was placed in her back. She was able to recover from surgery but was arrested. Her wrists were handcuffed to her bed. After she healed, she realized that she would never walk again. She was paralyzed from the waist down. After months of going through a painful journey of rehabilitation, she was transferred to prison.

GOD'S REDEMPTION

Lucy knew that she would be spending the rest of her life in prison. There were multiple charges against her. Pending burglary crimes were solved, and the stolen merchandise was found in her condo. She had to get around with a wheelchair.

Lucy was bored and hated prison life. She started reading various books and started reading the Bible. She repented for her sins and one day she got saved in church service that the prison held. She was changing from the inside out. As she started the sanctification process, she discovered that she could sing. She would practice singing daily, and people began requesting her to sing during the free time hour. God anointed her voice, and many people were delivered from strongholds. As Lucy sang, people wept, and they got saved afterward. Through God, Lucy did great exploits in prison. On her sentence day, she went from a life sentence to doing twenty-five years. God favored her, and she did her time.

Dear Heavenly Father,

I repent for stealing. Please remove the urge to steal out of my heart. I yield myself to you today. I humble myself before you. 2 Chronicles 7:14 says, "If my people, which are called by my name, shall humble themselves, and pray, and seek my face, and turn from their wicked ways; then will I hear from heaven, and will forgive their sin, and will heal their land." I decree that I will decrease so you can increase in me. I decree that I will be honest and walk uprightly before you. Thank you for answering this prayer in Jesus' name. Amen.

CHAPTER TWENTY SIX
Strife

BY KIMBERLY MOSES

Some people love to watch reality television. Some of the folks that are on these reality shows are full of strife. They are nothing but drama. There is no peace in their lives, they fight and argue all the time. As you mature, you will realize that strife leads to nothing good. Most people end up getting arrested or even dying. Merriam Webster defines strife as bitter sometimes violent conflict or dissension. It can also be an act of contention: fight, or struggle.[59] Proverbs 20:3 says, "It is an honour for a man to cease from strife: but every fool will be meddling." Strife can cost you everything. Now that we know what strife is let's look at the consequences.

CONSEQUENCES

1. Division

Wherever strife is present, there will be division. There will be no team work in marriage or the workplace. There will be no working together wherever strife is. The Bible tells us that a house divided against itself can't stand (Mark 3:25). How can two walk together unless they agree (Amos 3:3)? It is difficult to work with people that you don't get along with. The communication will be grievous. Arguments and tension may arise between you and the person that you have a fault with.

2. No Peace

There is no peace when there is strife. The atmosphere will be rocky and tense. You may not have peace internally because you are dealing with all kinds of thoughts in your mind. You may be thinking of taking revenge or getting your point across. You may be thinking about competing against the person that you have strife with. When you see or come around someone that you have a conflict with, then a fight can break out.

3. Violence

When there is strife, prepare for violence. When a person hates someone strife can easily enter. Proverbs 10:12 (ESV) says, "Hatred stirs up strife, but love covers all offenses." If you are full of strife, you will get violent if certain boundaries are crossed. If the person looks or says the wrong thing, it could set you off. Proverbs 29:22 (ESV) says, "A man of wrath stirs up strife, and one given to anger causes much transgression." The Bible warns us of acts of violence. Nothing good will come from it. James 1:20 says, "For the wrath of man worketh not the righteousness of God."

Now that we have discussed the consequences of strife let's look at how conflict can cost you everything.

TONY'S TESTIMONY

Tony grew up in the roughest neighborhoods. Every week on the news, someone was murdered. Tony wanted to be accepted, so he tried to join a gang. The only way to be initiated in was to kill someone. He couldn't target a random victim, but the leader had to choose the person for him. The leader's name was Carlos. He had beef or an issue with a rival gang leader named Joe. Tony's assignment was to kill Joe. Immediately his heart sank, and he was scared. "I don't want to kill anyone," he thought. I just wanted everyone to like me. He didn't know how he could even get close to Joe to make the kill. Carlos had everything planned out.

He wanted Tony to dress up like a delivery person and make the kill. Tony reluctantly agreed and decided to back out the morning of the plan. Hours passed then there was a knock at the door. It was someone who was associated with the gang that Tony wanted to join. Tony went outside and was punched in the stomach. A group of guys got him and brought him to Carlos. Carlos beat him badly. "You made me look like a fool. I don't like being stood up," he said. Tony promised to do what he wanted, so they let him go. However, Tony didn't have it in him. When he got back home, he ran away. He packed a bag and skipped school for a week. He thought that if he was out of sight, then he would be out of mind. The worst was about to happen.

Tony was cold, hungry, and running out of money. He decided to go back to his parent's house and face the consequences. When he arrived, he walked into a gruesome scene. His parents and little brother were murdered. "NO!" he cried out and fell to his knees sobbing. He knew that this was his fault. He was now an orphan and alone in the world. His family that he once loved is gone. He laid on the floor for hours crying and prayed to God. "Lord, I messed up. Forgive me. Help me."

GOD'S REDEMPTION

After he prayed that prayer, he gained strength to call the police. The detectives came and interviewed him. He told them everything that happened, and shortly after, Carlos and some other boys were arrested. Tony was placed in witness protection. After Carlos and the other boys who were involved were sentenced, Tony moved out of state. He lived with different foster families for a while. Some people didn't treat him right while others were genuinely concerned. One foster family took him to church. There he learned how to pray. He discovered what was meant for evil God can turn it around for his good.

Tony found out that God was calling him to minister to lost souls. Tony was afraid, but he embraced the Lord's plan for his life. Years later, Tony is educating the youth about gang violence. His goal is to prevent the youth from joining. He has been recognized by the mayor of his city. He has also appeared on numerous television shows and received many awards for his community work. You may have strife with someone. Just let it go because nothing good will come out of it. If you messed up in life or if someone hurt you, God will give you another chance and heal you.

Dear Heavenly Father,

I repent for being angry, violent, and bitter. I repent for hurting others by my actions. I don't want to live in strife anymore. Strengthen me to let it all go. I surrender my heart to you today. Jesus come into my heart and save me. Deliver me and cause me to be in your will. I want to live peaceably with all men. I want to be Spirit-filled, and Spirit-led. Bless me to produce the fruits of the Holy Spirit. Thank you for answering this prayer in Jesus' name. Amen.

CHAPTER TWENTY SEVEN
Ungodly Soul Ties

BY MAUDIA WASHINGTON

Have you ever experienced a soul tie? There are two types of soul ties: godly and ungodly. Ungodly soul ties are unhealthy relationships that can be destructive. If you have experienced an ungodly soul tie, then you understand the importance of identifying and breaking a soul tie before it's too late. According to Merriam-Webster dictionary, soul is a person's total self, a moving spirit, the moral and emotional nature of human beings and spiritual or moral force.[60] I want to highlight the part of the definition which states a person's total self. Total self is not part of the person but their total self which encompasses their heart, mind, emotions, physical nature, everything. According to Merriam-Webster dictionary, a tie is defined as to restrain from independence or freedom of action or choice: constrain by or as if by authority, influence, agreement, or obligation.[61]

The bible reference soul ties in Genesis 2:24 (ESV) it states, "Therefore, a man shall leave his father and his mother and hold fast to his wife and they shall become one flesh." This is how deep a soul tie can become one flesh which means there is no individuality anymore, but one person united together, unbreakable. Soul ties are commonly thought of between a man and a woman. This is not necessarily always the case. Soul ties can occur between parents, bosses, pastors, etc. Samuel 18:1 says, "And it came to pass, when he had made an end of speaking unto Saul, that the soul of Jonathan was knit with the soul of David, and Jonathan loved him as his own soul." Whoever can exert control over you can become a soul tie. I have personally experienced an ungodly soul tie in a relationship. I have experienced the highs and the very lows of it. My ungodly soul tie not only affected me but my business, family and social life. It almost cost me everything, but God saved me.

CONSEQUENCES

Now, that we have identified what a soul tie is, let's discuss the consequences of having ungodly soul ties. Ungodly Soul Ties can result in four things: Confusion, Idolatry, Rejection, and Deception. Soul ties can take you into another world, into a dark place, without you recognizing it and sometimes it too late.

1. Confusion

First, let's discuss confusion. According to 1 Corinthians 14:33, "God is not the author of confusion, but of peace." Remember, confusion is of the devil. God enjoys when his children are in peace. When you are at peace, you can hear God's voice clearer. When you are confused or distracted, it is hard to hear God's voice and heed to His commands.

Further, the bible states in 1 Peter 5:8, "Be sober-minded; be watchful. Your adversary the devil prowls around like a roaring lion, seeking someone to devour."

If your mind is not at rest, then you cannot be watchful. The devil knows this, and he knows how to distract you. So, you can turn your face from God. I have witnessed people who were amid confession. They couldn't make wise decisions and made a devasting decision which cost them years of frustration and confusion.

2. Idolatry

Second, now that we have touched on confusion lets discuss idolatry. According to Leviticus 19:4 (NIV) "Do not turn to idols or make metal gods for yourselves. I am the Lord your God." According to Exodus 20:3,5 (NIV), "You shall have no other gods before me...You shall not bow down to them or worship them; for I the Lord your God, am a jealous God..." Sometimes people do not recognize that they are idolizing a person and putting them before God. When a person consumes so much of your time and your life that you do not have time for God, you are idolizing them. As the scriptures stated you shall have no other gods before our Lord God and that God is a jealous God.

3. Rejection

The third consequence is rejection. Rejection is the feeling of unworthiness by another person. Rejection hurts to the core and can make you feel not good enough. No one should have to feel this way, especially not a child of God. According to 1 Peter 2:4 (NIV), "As you come to him, the living Stone-rejected by humans but chosen by God precious to him." In addition, according to Isaiah 49:15 (NIV), "Can a mother forget the baby at their breast and have no compassion on the child she has borne? Though she may forget, I will not forget you!" God is saying men may turn their backs on you, but God will never leave you. God will get your attention at any cost. I have seen people who were rejected have low self-esteem, settle for anything, and never achieved their God-given purpose.

4. Deception

Fourth, Deception is a consequence of ungodly soul ties. According to Ephesians 5:6 (NIV), "Let no one deceive you with empty words, for because of such things God's wrath comes on those who are disobedient." Also, in Romans 16:18 it states, "For such people are not serving our Lord Christ, but their own appetite by smooth talk and flattery they deceive the minds of naïve people." Ungodly soul ties can be manipulators out to take advantage of you. They may use smooth words and empty promises to persuade you. Some may use bible verses and say that they are sent from God. Focus on their actions and not their words. Focus on the fruit that they bear. Is it good fruit? Words can be deceptive. Actions are not. I have seen many people become prey to manipulators.

MAUDIA'S TESTIMONY

We have identified the four consequences of ungodly soul ties. Let me explain how ungodly soul ties almost cost me everything. Have you ever prayed hard for years and your prayers finally manifested? This is how my soul tie began. I prayed for a partner. My prayer request was very specific, including his height, childhood background, educational background, occupation, amount of years in his occupation, parental upbringing, previous marital status, physical appearance, and religious background. I laid my petition before God for over ten years, and He granted by request. When I first met him, I was in disbelief that God sent me a person with the specificity I requested. I was internally grateful and did not want to let God down or mess up the relationship. I did everything to keep him. I did not give myself sexually to him, but emotionally, I desired to be perfect.

I felt as if I had to do everything right. I had to say the right things. I had to look a certain way. I had to be the best representation of myself as possible. I had to laugh at his cue and be present at his call. God gave me this gift, and I did not want to lose it. He was very good at words, but his actions were inconsistent. I became confused because he did not bear good fruit. He completely absorbed my mind. He became my idol. I could not function throughout the day if I did not communicate with him. This was a daily cycle. I began to seek psychic advice, and I felt a heavy spirit over me. I felt deceived because of the many unfulfilled promises. My mind was not at rest, and my life was in shambles. There were red flags, and my spirit knew something was not right, but he was my idol. We were attached, and we had a bond. The more I turned to psychics, the more I pushed God out. He had a stronghold over me. I was addicted. He was my drug.

The closer we became, the less time that I had for God. God was an afterthought. My family became very concerned because I was not myself. I stopped socializing. I finally heard a voice that said, "Surrender it to me." Surrendering is a form of weakness to me. I continued to try to problem solve, but my situation got worse. God spoke again, "Surrender it to me. Lay it at the altar." During my struggle, God continued to ask me to surrender it to Him. I said, "No, God. I prayed for him, and You gave him to me. He is mine." God said, "Surrender it." I was against it and wanted to do it my way. God reminded me of the story of Abraham and Sarah. They both wanted a child for a very long time.

God promised Sarah that she would have a child in her old age. The promise did not come about quickly enough, and they thought God forgot. Sarah and Abraham conspired to conceive a child with Hagar. This was out of the will of God. Eventually, Isaac was born to Sarah and Abraham. This is the son that Sarah and Abraham both wanted for many years. One day God told Abraham to sacrifice Isaac. Abraham immediately obeyed and did not question God. Right before Abraham was about to kill his son, God stopped him. God tested Abraham's faith. Abraham was willing to sacrifice his son. After God continuing asking me to give my situation to him, I finally surrendered and left it at the altar.

GOD'S REDEMPTION

With my ungodly soul tie, I almost fell, but God caught me. The devil thought that he had me, but God said, "Do not touch my anointed ones; do my prophets no harm (Psalm 105:15 (NIV)." God had me in the palm of his hands. According to Romans 12:2 (NIV), "Do not conform to the pattern of this world but be transformed by the renewing of your mind. Then you will be able to test and approve what God's will is--his good, pleasing and perfect will." God had to renew my mind. I had to stop the negative thinking. I started reading the bible from Genesis to Revelation. Once I cut my soul tie and surrendered it to God. I did not look back. I had to push forward. According to 2 Corinthians 5:17, "Therefore if any man is in Christ, he is a new creature: old things are passed away; behold, all things have become new."

I had to let the old me die. I had to stop the cycle and ended the relationship. I had to remember my dreams and establish new goals. I had to envision myself in a new light. I had to see myself healthier and beautiful. God told me that he would give me the secret petitions of my heart. God began to give me new visions and promises. He began to do a new thing in me. He gave me book ideas. I began to write three books, two articles, started another business, and finished goals that I started years ago. My personal and professional life began to turn around. I began to spend more time with my family and friends. I repented to God. I apologized to my family and prayed for that person. God removed confusion and rejection. He gave me glory for ashes.

Unexpected people began to show up in my life that I would not have never met; influential people and well-known people. I started to get unbelievable favor. God revealed the significance of Jeremiah 29:11(NIV), "For I know the plans I have for you declares the Lord. Plans to prosper you and not harm you. Plans to give you hope and a future." God began to minister to me and reminded me of all my prayer requests. Lastly, God revealed the reason for my soul tie. My soul tie was brought in my life to get my attention. God gave me something that I wanted and then took it away, so I could deeply seek His face. That thorn and affliction allowed me to have a greater connection and encounter with God. I trusted Him, and I loved God more than my soul tie. According to Job 11:13-15 (CEV), "Surrender your heart to God, turn to him in prayer and give up your sins, -even those you do in secret. Then you won't be ashamed; you will be confident and fearless." I broke free and you can too. The adversary thought that he had me, but God saved me.

Heavenly Father,

I come boldly before the throne of grace. I thank You for breaking yokes. I thank You for renewing my mind, giving me a new song to sing and for breaking soul ties. Philippians 4:6 (NIV) says, "Do not be anxious about anything, but in every situation, by prayer and petition, with thanksgiving, present your requests to God." Lord God, I will follow You and not be anxious. I will wait on Your command and allow You to bring into my life healthy relationships and remove ungodly relationships. Thank You for new beginnings and breakthroughs. God, you sit high and look low. You know which path for me to take. You said that You knew me before the foundation of the world and Your promise shall not return to You void. Today is the day that I am a new me. I am no longer a victim to my situation. I am glorious. I am David and have defeated Goliath. You have turned my situation around. What the devil meant for bad, God meant for good. Thank You for deliverance. I rebuke confusion and the feeling of rejection. You are not the author of confusion. I rejoice in Your name and Glory. I repent for not putting You first in my life, and I am sorry for not spending time with You. Without You, I am nothing, but with You I am everything. In the name of Jesus. Amen.

CHAPTER TWENTY EIGHT
Witchcraft

BY LASHANA LLOYD

Witchcraft is a term that is commonly used today, but do people really understand the full effects of it? According to the Merriam-Webster Dictionary, witchcraft is defined as the use of sorcery or magic. It also involves communicating with the devil or a familiar spirit. [62.] From a Biblical standpoint, Deuteronomy 18:10-12 (NLT) says, "... And do not let your people practice fortune-telling, or use sorcery, or interpret omens, or engage in witchcraft, or cast spells, or function as mediums or psychics, or call forth the spirits of the dead. Anyone who does these things is detestable to the Lord." Not knowing the harmful effects of witchcraft can cause more harm than you will ever know. I can testify to that because witchcraft almost cost me everything.

CONSEQUENCES

Now that you understand what witchcraft is, I will now discuss a few of the numerous consequences that could happen to someone who is operating in witchcraft:

1. No Salvation

First, those who use witchcraft, who do not repent and turn from this evil use, will not enter heaven. Galatians 5:19-21(NIV) says, "The acts of the flesh are obvious: sexual immorality, impurity and debauchery; idolatry and witchcraft; hatred, discord, jealousy, fits of rage, selfish ambition, dissensions, factions and envy; drunkenness, orgies, and the like. I warn you, as I did before, that those who live like this will not inherit the kingdom of God." The Greek word for witchcraft is pharmakeia.[63] In the English translation, this is where the word pharmacy[64] comes from. When used and/or performed, witchcraft satisfies the lust of the flesh (1 John 2:16-NIV). This is made clear that since witchcraft is not of the Father, and it comes from the enemy, those who choose to use witchcraft will not be able to enter the kingdom of God because God's salvation will not be granted.

2. Witchcraft Becomes Parallel to Rebellion

Next, witchcraft and rebellion are fatal to the kingdom of God. The first part of 1 Samuel 15:23 says, "For rebellion is as the sin of witchcraft, and stubbornness is as iniquity and idolatry." When explaining this, it can be said that walking in rebellion can be compared to operating in witchcraft. When you make the choice to get involved in witchcraft, you have just decided to disobey God. Just like rebellion, witchcraft will lead you away from God and will place you on a path that could lead you to physical and spiritual destruction.

3. Reap Your Own Curses

Lastly, witchcraft will result in a person reaping their own curses. Galatians 6:7-8 (NIV) says, "Do not be deceived: God cannot be mocked. A man reaps what he sows. Whoever sows to please their flesh, from the flesh will reap destruction; whoever sows to please the Spirit, from the Spirit will reap eternal life." Apostle Paul begins the opening of this Scripture by saying, "Do not be deceived" which is another way of saying, "Do not allow yourselves to be taken advantage of or be tricked by someone else." There are so many people around the world who have fallen prey to being tricked by witchcraft, and most of the ones who are deceiving, and tricking others do not have a conscience about what they are doing.

Satan is raising up false prophets, witches, warlocks, Satanists, and witch doctors every day to do his dirty work. He will have those who are operating in witchcraft believe that they will not reap what they have sown. The enemy will also deceive others who perform witchcraft into believing that they can invoke evil powers on others and still reap good things. They feel like there are no consequences for their actions, and they are fine with that. This is the deception that is increasing greatly in the world today pertaining to witchcraft.

LASHANA'S TESTIMONY

Now that you have read about some of the consequences of witchcraft, I will now share my testimony about how witchcraft, at one point in time, almost cost me my destiny. Some years ago, I remember I befriended this woman who was on fire for Christ and doing great things for God's kingdom. We instantly connected because of a lot of the similarities that we shared, especially our love for God. I would support her when she would have prayer calls/meetings and gatherings she would have at her house with her friends. This was the divine connection I had always prayed to the Father for, but the answer to this prayer between us was short lived.

A couple of months after I met this woman, she told me that she was going out of the country for a couple of weeks to do missionary work. One of the people she met while she was on this missionary trip was a "prophet" that she met on a social media site that we were on. She was secretly dating him before she left the states. When she returned to the states, I thought that things were going to be the same as they were before she left, but they were not. When I wanted to make plans to hang out or fellowship, she declined because the man that she was dating wanted her to spend all her time with him. If we did fellowship with each other, this man would contact her (via texting or calling her) throughout the entire time we were having lunch. In my spirit, I felt that something was not right about this man, but I never addressed my concerns to her about him.

Overtime, the controlling and deceptive ways of this man became even more obvious. If this woman and I were talking on the phone, and this man was with her, the entire conversation would have to take place with her being on speakerphone so that he could hear what we were talking about. While I was on the phone with her, he always had "a word" to give to me, but the words that he gave to me were either false, or he was receiving his information from another source (the enemy) instead of the Source (God). There were things I had told this woman about my calling and purpose that she would go back and tell this man about behind my back. He was forcing her to do it-she was betraying me. This man would release words to me about my business, finances, and ministry. Not once did I question him or seek the Father on what he was saying because I thought that he was this great prophet. But, not only was he a wolf in sheep's clothing, he was also a warlock (a male witch). He had converted my former friend into a witch.

Overtime, this woman became aggressive, like the man she was dating. They both tried to consume all my time especially when I was trying to prepare to walk in my assignment. It even went as far as my former friend giving me his phone number. He would text me several times a day, five days a week, when my former friend would be at work. He now had complete control over her. Because he had control over her, he wanted to have control over everyone who was connected with her.

Instead of me seeking God about whether the words this man released over my life were true, I came into agreement with them. This was the beginning of the end for me. Receiving information about me from my former friend was how this man was able to "prophelie" to me, resulting in me being deceived and manipulated even more. There was one time, I allowed this man and woman to come over to a previous home that I was staying in. Upon them arriving, this man did not waste any time giving me false prophetic words. I allowed this man to speak about the man God said was going to be my husband. The reason why he knew the information that he did know was because my former friend had told him. He started on the positive side, but shortly afterward, he started telling me about this woman that this man was involved with, which now had me in a place of confusion (which was a part his plan all along).

Shortly after this encounter, I started having dreams about female demonic spirits being around this man that God had told me for years was going to be my husband. Instead of me canceling the dreams and praying for this man, I gave up. I was no longer hopeful or interested in what God had been telling me for years about him. As a result of that, I ended up losing my future husband before God was able to bring everything to pass between us. It was all because of the lies and false prophetic words I allowed myself to come into agreement with.

Every area of my life I allowed this man to speak over became ruined. My finances were heavily depleted, and my business was slow with moving forward. Because I let the two of them into my house, things started breaking down in my house back-to-back behind each other (that had never broken down before for the duration of the time I was living in this residence). I almost became homeless. All these mishaps were taking place in my life because of the curses these two were now preying over me and the evil altars they had created against me. This man even tried to destroy my laptop (while I was working on my manuscript for my book) so that the testimony that God had for me to write about would not be released. Feeling that I've taken all that I could take from them, I severed all ties. They did not sever ties with me.

This couple had gotten used to controlling and manipulating me. They wanted it to continue. After I blocked all access they had to me, they started astral projecting themselves in my dreams. In one of these dreams, the woman and I were arguing back and forth with each other. When I got tired of arguing with her, I walked up to her, placed my fingers in the middle of her forehead, and said, "Get out of my life, and stay out of my life in Jesus' Name." After I said this, she cried, turned around and walked away. The dream shifted, and I was now in a kitchen area of somebody else's house that I did not recognize. A man was wearing what looked like a full-face wrestling mask that had an orange bolt going down one of the eyes of the mask that was sitting at a kitchen table. Although I could not see his face, I knew it was the warlock. He was sitting at the table holding a white envelope that had my name written on it as well as some other information written underneath my name. When I sought the Father for the interpretation of this part of the dream, He told me, "He has your destiny sealed up."

GOD'S REDEMPTION

Shortly after I received the revelation about this dream, I prayed to the Father as to what I needed to do with this couple trying to redirect my course in life and my purpose. He led me to a minister who gave specific instructions in the area of witchcraft. The minister said that if I had received a false prophetic word from anyone who was a false prophet, go on a fast, pray against every false word that was spoken over me (as well as every curse or spell that was placed over me), and use Scriptures to combat with what I was praying for. This minister also prayed that the curses would be broken, for the ungodly soul ties to be broken from this couple, and that the blood of Jesus would cleanse, heal, and deliver me.

Shortly after I followed these instructions, I had another dream. This couple was in this dream, but this time, they were standing in a far-off distance from me. For whatever reason, they were not able to walk towards me, or do anything to me. The woman never looked at me. Her head was held down the entire time. I could tell that the man was angry, and he wanted to attack me, but he never did because something (or Someone-the protection of God) was stopping him from doing so. I was able to walk freely past them in this dream, and they could not do anything to me. The only thing the man could do was yell insults at me- as an attempt to get me to operate in the flesh- but every time he insulted me, I responded with the love of Jesus; this made him angrier. From that dream, I knew that they had lost their evil powers and control from over me. The witchcraft they once had over me was now broken.

Since that time, I became a Christian author, blogger, writer, and life coach for women. I have been getting interviewed about my business, and ministry. I am in the process of getting prepared for speaking engagements. After this experience, I no longer disable my discernment. If there is a check in my spirit about someone, I take heed to that. I pray about the people who now come into my life and take heed to what the Holy Spirit reveals to me about them because I will have so much at stake if I do not.

God is so awesome! He redeemed and restored me from that which the enemy tried to use against me in the form of witchcraft. Just as God sends people along your path to help you with your assignment, the enemy will also send people along your path to try to destroy it. Therefore, it is important to do what is stated in 1 John 4:1 (NIV) which says, "Dear friends, do not believe every spirit, but test the spirits to see whether they are from God, because many false prophets have gone out into the world." Witchcraft almost cost me everything, but the Father, through His grace and mercy, healed, delivered, and restored my life, assignment, and destiny back to Him.

Dear Heavenly Father,

I come before you in repentance of salvation. I have been operating in witchcraft, and I know that this is displeasing to You. Please deliver me from operating in witchcraft and all of the evil powers connected to witchcraft that is in the form of, but not limited to, curses, words curses, control, mind control, manipulation, domination, intimidation, spells, voodoo, hexes, vexes, magic, astral projection, potions, destruction, death, and anything else I have not identified that You would consider being the works of the enemy. Let your grace and mercy come upon me this day and consume me. Please cleanse me, and my current and future generations with the power, authority, and resurrection blood of Jesus. Set me free from witchcraft and redirect my life to where I need to be in you in Jesus' Name. Amen.

About The Authors

Kimberly Moses started off her ministry as Kimberly Hargraves. She is highly sought after as a prophetic voice, intercessor and prolific author. There is no doubt that she has a global mandate on her life to serve the nations of the world by spreading the Gospel of Jesus Christ. She has a quickly expanding worldwide healing and deliverance ministry. Kimberly Moses wears many hats to fulfill the call God has placed on her life as an entrepreneur over several businesses including her own personal brand Rejoice Essentials which promotes the Gospel of Jesus Christ. She also serves as a life coach and mentor to many women. She is also the loving mother of two wonderful children. She is married to Tron. Kimberly has dedicated her life to the work of ministry and to serve others under the call God has placed over her life. Kimberly currently resides in South Carolina.

She is a very anointed woman of God who signs, miracles, and wonders follow. The miraculous and incessant testimonies attributed to her ministry are incalculable, with many reporting physical and mental healing, financial breakthroughs, debt cancellations, and other favorable outcomes. She is known across the globe as a servant who truly labors on behalf of God's people through intercession.

She is the author of The Following:

"Overcoming Difficult Life Experiences with Scriptures and Prayers"

"Overcoming Emotions with Prayers"

"Daily Prayers That Bring Changes"

"In Right Standing,"

"Obedience Is Key,"

"Prayers That Break The Yoke Of The Enemy: A Book Of Declarations,"

"Prayers That Demolish Demonic Strongholds: A Book Of Declarations,"

"Work Smarter. Not Harder. A Book Of Declarations For The Workforce,"

"Set The Captives Free: A Book Of Deliverance."

"Pray More Challenge"

"Walk By Faith: A Daily Devotional"

"Empowering The New Me: Fifty Tips To Becoming A Godly Woman"

"School of the Prophets: A Curriculum For Success"

"8 Keys To Accessing The Supernatural"

"Conquering The Mind: A Daily Devotional"

"Enhancing The Prophetic In You"

"The ABCs of The Prophetic: Prophetic Characteristics"

"Wisdom is the Principle Thing: A Daily Devotional"

You can find more about Kimberly at www.kimberlyhargraves.com

Prophet Joy Martin is the founder and senior pastor of Bethel Ministry Center. She is not called to do ministry in a traditional way. As a radical trailblazer, Pastor Joy operates in the dimension of radical faith, and she radically loves Jesus. She believes that all believers should operate in the "full gospel" of Jesus Christ (Repentance, Salvation, Healing, Deliverance and the Prophetic Word being released into the earth).

As a Prophet called to the Nations, Prophet Martin imparts biblical truths. Her ministry operates in the realm of the Supernatural, Healing, and Deliverance. She partners with the Holy Spirit and assists God's children in being set free from being "demonized" or "infected" by demons. She constantly reminds believers that Jesus Christ came to set the captives free!

Prophet Martin launched her television show, A Place of Transformation in 2018 on the All Nations TV Network on the ROKU platform. She is also the author of the International best-selling book, "Are You A Giant Slayer?" Over the years, Prophet Martin has spoken at churches, conferences, and women's retreats; however, the most humbling and honorable experience was to preach her grandmother's funeral! Pastor Martin and her two children reside in the Philadelphia area.

Website: joymartinministries.com
Phone: 267.777.8119
Facebook: Joy Martin Ministries

Coretta Moore Kelsey is from Eldorado, Arkansas. She resides in Nashville, Tennessee. Coretta has always been a Woman of Faith. Coretta is always witnessing to someone about how God has changed her life. Coretta does Periscope and YouTube videos as the Lord leads. You can find some of her testimonies there.

Coretta has worked for many years in the field of nursing. She has been the Founder and Owner of Coretta Cares Inc. since 2015. Coretta attended Volunteer State Community College in Gallatin, Tennessee for Pre-Nursing. She also received a certificate to become a Certified Nursing Assistant in 2004. Coretta later went on to attend Nashville College of Medical Careers in Madison, TN to become a Medical Assistant in 2007. Coretta has also attended the School of The Prophets by Prophetess Kimberly Moses.

Coretta loves doing ministry, enjoying family time and traveling. Coretta spent a lot of time talking to God as a child. She had to endure so much growing up and even as an adult, but she refused to give up. God spared her life several times throughout the years, and she is just blessed to be here to tell others about it. She is always ready and willing to share her testimonies so that people may have hope and trust God. Revelations 12:11 says, "And they overcame him by the blood of the lamb, and by the word of their testimonies; and they loved not their lives unto death."

You can contact Coretta by email or phone.

Email is LovingJesus1st@icloud.com
cell number 615-927-2804

Coretta_Kelsey on Periscope

Facebook
Godisolatedme Tochangeme
Coretta Moore

YouTube
Coretta Moore

DeWanda Ann Samuel is a native of Florence, South Carolina. She is a servant leader called by God and a prophetic voice of the 21st century. She possesses a genuine passion and deep love for Jesus and the "Word" of God. DeWanda received Jesus Christ as her personal Lord and Savior as a young adult at the tender age of twenty-four years old while living in Grafenwoehr, Germany. Since then, she has been standing on God's word and God's promises for almost twenty-five years. Her life's story is a testimony to God's unconditional steadfast love and His enduring grace and mercy.

DeWanda is dedicated and determined to live by the Word of God in all areas of her life. She believes in the power of prayer and is a gifted anointed prayer warrior. In February 2017, she answered God's called again and became the founder of the Worship & Warfare Prayer Chambers prayer ministry which is founded on Isaiah 58:12. This scripture says, "Your people will rebuild the ancient ruins and will raise up the age-old foundations; you will be called a Repairer of Broken Walls, Restorer of Street with Dwellings." DeWanda is a sought-after intercessor and prayer strategist. During the last three years she serves as a Lead Intercessor at The Global Dynamic Prayer Ministry partnering with and praying with people from around the world from Japan to the Caribbean. She believes that God has entrusted her with a fruitful ministry that will transform lives but especially the lives of other fathers, husbands, sons, brothers, mothers, grandmothers, daughters, sisters, aunts, nieces, and sister-friends.

DeWanda is a Distinguished Honor Graduate of DeVry University. She holds a Bachelor of Science Degree in Computer Engineering. She has served her government as a Civil Servant for the last fifteen years and twelve of those years at the United States Patent & Trademark Office as a Computer Engineer/Patent Examiner. She is a licensed Cosmetologist. Presently, she resides in DMV area in Northern Virginia with her family. In her spare time, she enjoys her favorite hobbies, babysitting her grandbaby and refurbishing old furniture. One of her favorite life-giving scripture is Joshua 1:7 "Be strong and very courageous. Be careful to obey all the law my servant Moses gave you; do not turn from it to the right or to the left, that you may be successful wherever you go."

Contact info:
Email: worshipnwarprayer57@gmail.com
Email:dewanda.samuel5778@gmail.com
Facebook info: Anne Mcelveen
Periscope: @ShamarWarrior/AnneSamuel

Joyce Hope was born in Accomac County, Virginia. At the age of four years old, in pursuit of a better life for herself and her children, her mother relocated to Brooklyn, New York. At the tender age of fourteen years old, Joyce accepted Jesus Christ as her personal Savior. She became a member of Mt. Zion Pentecostal Holiness Church, where she received her Christian foundation and teaching.

In 1988, Joyce joined the Pentecostal House of Prayer of Deliverance under the tutelage of Chief Prelate Bishop McKinley Green, in Brooklyn, New York. Joyce attended Bethel Bible Institute from Fall 1991 through Spring 1997. She is currently pursuing a Degree in Theology from the Dominion Global Bible Institute and Seminary.

Joyce is an ordained Elder and the mother of two adult children. She also has an identical twin sister who shares her love and passion for prayer and writing. They are new authors of several books. You may contact Joyce @ joycehope7@gmail.com, or on social media on Facebook @ Joyce Hope, Periscope @ Joyce Hope2, $ReJoyce7 on cash app and paypal .me/ReJoyce7

LaShana Lloyd is a Christian author, blogger, speaker, and life coach for women. She helps women, from all walks of life, become encouraged, inspired, and empowered so that their confidence can become stronger. In 2016, LaShana started Faith Led Life and Faith Led Life Coaching, LLC. She was amazed at how excited people were searching to improve their lives, the different areas of their lives, and the lives of others. LaShana's vision is to prepare the hearts of women to receive the Glory of Jesus and teach them the importance of establishing a relationship with God through the Holy Spirit with encouragement and inspiration. Her mission is to prepare women by nourishing their souls with the words spoken or written that will lead them to or back to God with a passion driven purpose to inspire and encourage women to walk purposely in their calling. Her mission equips them to receive the Father's glory.

LaShana is being led by faith to do the things that must be done for God's glory. It is her prayer that her ministry will lead other women back to God with the words that she writes and speaks. It is also LaShana's desire that women will find encouragement in her because of her walk with God- which will prepare them to receive more of God or receive Him for the first time. LaShana strongly believes that women of faith will come from her ministry and prepare them to do greater work for God's kingdom.

AUTHOR

In 2018, LaShana was featured in an anthology entitled "You Have No Idea the Hell I've Been Through: 22 Women Who Pushed from Pain to Purpose." In this powerful, bestselling, book, LaShana discusses how she witnessed abuse in her home, being sexually abused as a child, and her experience with being blackballed from the military. With all glory going to God, she was able to forgive, be healed from her past, and allow what she went through to contribute greatly to the purpose the Father had for her. For more information about this book, and how to order, go to www.youhavenoideabooks.com.

Also, in 2018, LaShana released an amazing book entitled What's Blocking Your Confidence? Effective Tools to Conquer Your Fears." Released by Rejoicing Essential Publishing, "What's Blocking Your Confidence? Effective Tools to Conquer Your Fears" provides important information about fear, how to conquer fear, and how to walk in the confidence that God has given you. LaShana becomes transparent and gives her testimony about how she was once bound by fear, in different ways, and how God delivered her from it. "What's Blocking Your Confidence? Effective Tools to Conquer Your Fears" is available on Amazon, Barnes, and Noble, and www.confidenceblocker.com

CHRISTIAN LIFE COACHING FOR WOMEN

As a Christian life coach, LaShana inspires her clients to seek the Lord's will in their lives and align their lives with God's plan. She helps her clients reach certain goals or give encouragement to them when they are facing changes or transition in their lives. She also uses coaching knowledge, proficiencies, and tools to assist her clients in finding their talents and gifts to benefit a greater purpose and uses prayer in addition to traditional coaching tools to assist in removal of obstacles presented by the enemy (Satan). LaShana is originally from Clio, South Carolina, but currently resides in Northern Virginia. Learn more about LaShana at www.faithledlife.com.

Email: info@faithledlife.com

Facebook:@faithledlifeofficial

Instagram: @faithledlifeofficial

Pinterest: @faithledlife

LinkedIn: @Faithledlife

Melissa Portis grew up as an only child. Her father was in the military which caused them to travel often. As a result, Melissa lived in Europe and different parts of the world. She became well cultured and able to relate to people from different backgrounds and all walks of life. As an adult, she attended Lincoln College and graduated with a degree in Liberal Arts and Sciences.

Melissa went on to become a flight attendant for a major airline for several years. In 2006, She gave birth to a beautiful girl named Mariah. After taking some time off, Melissa decided to go back into the workforce and work for a modeling and talent company in Chicago. This was a fun and rewarding career for Melissa. At this time in her life, she took every opportunity to learn about the Lord. Other talent scouts and herself would get together, worship, and orchestrate prayer meetings. This was the beginning of her spiritual awakening.

Melissa has become a powerful prophetic intercessor. She believes that being a part of a ministry is not just about being a member and warming the pews every Sunday; but it's about growth, development, cultivating and contributing. She's a mighty woman of God with a pure heart and has genuine compassion for others.

Contact information
Email: Interceding4U.Melissa@gmail.com
Periscope: iLoveFavor
Facebook book Mel Lissa

Yolanda Samuels is an author, prophetic intercessor, dreamer, Bible study teacher, Sunday School teacher, Youth church teacher, an usher, and an active member of Varnville Church of God. She has an anointing to teach on her life. She is also an entrepreneur and has a tutoring service called Excel In Learning that she started in 2016. She tutors Elementary aged children in all subjects. She works as a paraprofessional and is passionate about helping children learn no matter how challenging it may be.

She is a United States Navy veteran where she served for 14 years. She was an Information Systems Technician (IT). She served in the war on terrorism during 911 on September of 2001. She deployed to Kandahar, Afghanistan to set up communication services for the troops who would utilize them for the duration. She received numerous awards in her military career. She separated from the military in 2009 as an E-6 (Petty Officer First Class). She received an honorable discharge.

She loves learning and teaching others. Especially young children. She has a Bachelor of Business Administration with a concentration in Information's System Technician. She also has a Bachelor's and a Masters of Arts in Early Childhood Education and degree in Early Childhood. She has a five-year background in Childcare where she worked as an infant, toddler teacher, pre-k teacher, and preschool teacher. She also was an Assistant Director and Acting Director.

She has endured many trials in her life, but God uses them for her to strengthen and minister to others by advising and praying for them. She is a loving wife to Joseph and an auntie of seven. Yolanda is the daughter of Nathaniel and Pearly Johnson. She has two brothers and two sisters. They currently reside in South Carolina. If you would like more information about Yolanda Samuels, you can follow her on https://www.facebook.com/yolanda.jacobs2 and Excel In Learning Tutoring Services https://www.facebook.com/Excel-In-Learning-Tutoring-Services-5288022341125398/

You can check out her blog at https://www.facebook.com/It-Cost-Me-Everything-350481109139367/?hc_location=ufi

Zolisha L Ware gave her life to Christ at age twenty-six just a few weeks short of her 27th birthday on August 28, 2004. Zolisha has been a member of Integrity Deliverance Ministry since that date. It wasn't long after giving her life, she received the gift of Holy Ghost during the church's 9th-anniversary service for Integrity Deliverance Ministry. Zolisha became the Praise & Worship Leader for the ministry in April 2005 where she has continued to hold that role still today. Sometime after being made the Praise & Worship Leader, she was also charged to lead the Dance Ministry within the church. Zolisha believes her most prized possession is her relationship unto the Lord, and you can see the evidence within her singing and dancing unto the Lord.

Before a relationship with the Lord, Zolisha was robbed of her education by anger and bitterness due to life struggles of being a teenage mother. However, once she became under the healing power of Jesus Christ, the spirit of the Lord directed Zolisha in 2007 to pursue her education. Shortly after the ushering of the Spirit of the Lord to get her education, Zolisha found out that she should have already received her high school diploma. However, since it was so many years after that period, Zolisha was required to take two online tests. One which was within English and the other within Science to receive a fully accredited high school diploma.

She completed both tests online quickly. After completing the classes, Zolisha was awarded her High School diploma in

September 2007 from Excel High School located in Plymouth, MN. Once she was able to accomplish her high school diploma, she was continually driven by the Spirit of the Lord to further her education by signing up for college. Therefore, in the spring of 2008, Zolisha began to attend Lincoln College-Normal IL location. She received her Associates in Arts in 2011, and three years later she received her Bachelors in Liberal Arts. Once Zolisha obtained her bachelor's degree, she thought she had completed her studies. However, the drive for education continued to burn heavily within her. Therefore, after consulting with the Lord, she enrolled in Liberty University located in Lynchburg VA in August of 2014.

A year or so after being enrolled within the Master program in May of 2015, Zolisha encountered a supernatural dream that lasted for three night. Within that dream, Zolisha was tested on things that the Lord had delivered her from like greed, anger, sexual immorality, hate, and perversion. At the end of that dream, Zolisha was given a mandate straight from heaven to birth an outreach program geared toward helping women to be more Christ-centered. Thus, Safe Haven Women Outreach was birth. Zolisha is the founder and President of the community outreach ministry and currently the program services the Bloomington-Normal IL Community area. Safe Haven Women Outreach also has an online presence, and you can find the outreach on Facebook by simply searching the name. Anyone regardless if they live in the Bloomington-Normal IL Community or not can follow the page by simply liking the page.

During Zolisha development of the outreach, she continued to pursue her education but at a slower pace while launching the outreach. SHWO's first day of service was April 16, 2016. The program has been said to bring the deliverance power of God and to transform every life that steps within the thresholds of the outreach program. Once the program was fully up and running, Zolisha continued to pursue her education with Liberty University where she received a Masters degree in Executive Leadership in March of 2017. Zolisha has stated that her education in the secular world has concluded and now has a mandate from heaven to learn all she can concerning the Kingdom of God. Zolisha believes that in God learning never stops. She believes we all should be striving to have the mind of Christ by studying all we can to help us be more like Jesus.

Contact Info:

Facebook//Instagram: Zolisha Ware

Email: infozlware@gmail.com

Facebook//Instagram: Safe Haven Women Outreach

Email: safehavenwomenoutreach@gmail.com

Jennifer M. Jackson is originally from Panama City, Florida. From the time she was five years old, she has been involved in ministry. She sings in her local church's Start Light Choir, a member of the Ushers Youth Department, Youth Secretary and a member of the Youth Choir. She dedicated her life to Christ at the age of twelve years old and has been serving ever since. She currently serves in the United States Army with over twenty-two years of military service. Joining straight out of high school, her military travels has opened the door for her to serve in different ministries cultivating her love for Christ. During these assignments, she worked with both the Children and Teen Ministries. She is serving as both a ministry head and teacher. She realized during serving in these ministries her passion for working with the youth and inspiring them to be all they can be in Christ. She is also a praise dance leader and is currently a Minister in Training (MIT) at Praise Temple Full Gospel Baptist Church located in El Paso, TX under the leadership of Bishop Harrison B. Johnson.

She serves as a Logistic NCO in the United States Army. Throughout her time in the military her assignments have taken her to Hawaii, Hunter Army Airfield, GA, Kaiserslautern, Germany, Israel, Tbilisi, Georgia (the country), Italy, Fort Hood, TX and to her present assignment in Fort Bliss, TX. During her military service she has deployed to Iraq in support Operation Iraqi Freedom (OEF) and Afghanistan in support of both Operation Enduring Freedom (OEF) and Operation Resolute Support (ORS). She knows that each assignment she has been on, God has placed her there not only to grow but to empower others. She strives to inspire others to not only grow in their walk with Christ but to look beyond their present state and to know that the best is yet to come in their lives. She is credentialed in the Department of Defense Sexual Assault Advocate and Credentialed Advocate (CA). She received a National Organization for Victims Assistance (NOVA) Honorary Award for her timeless efforts in the advance of crime victims' rights.

She has a Bachelor's Degree in Early Childhood Education from Liberty University. She has one son named Johnathan who has followed her throughout her military career as well. She is a collector of dolphins because of their natural smile and innate nature to be a helper. She loves bowling, writing, reading decorating and her favorite pastime is football.

Contact Information:
Jennifer M Jackson
Trulyblessed1977@yahoo.com
Instagram and Periscope: iamakingskid

Dr. Maudia Washington, MBA, JD, DBA

Dr. Washington is a devoted Christian and believes strongly in continuing to seek after God. Dr. Washington grew up in the Church of God In Christ (COGIC).

Dr. Maudia Washington graduated from Southern Illinois University with a Bachelor of Arts degree in Administration of Justice with a minor in Sociology. She attended Robert Morris University where she graduated with a Master of Business Administration. Dr. Washington has a Doctor of Business Administration in International Business and graduated from Michigan State University School of Law with a Juris Doctor in Business Law. Dr. Washington is currently pursuing a Master of Laws degree in Real Estate Litigation.

Dr. Washington is an Attorney who is licensed to practice in Illinois state courts. Ms. Washington is also licensed to practice in all three Illinois Federal District Courts: The United States District Court for the Northern District of Illinois, The United States District Court for the Central District of Illinois and The United States District Court for the Southern District of Illinois. In addition, Ms. Washington is also licensed in the United States Tax Court.

Dr. Washington is the owner of Washington Law Offices. Washington Law Offices are located in Chicago, Illinois and Elgin, Illinois. Her practice focuses on complex civil litigation, business law, employment discrimination, contract disputes, real estate litigation, copyrights infringement, and other civil matters.

Ms. Washington was a speaker at the 111th Church of God In Christ Holy Convocation Conference in St. Louis, Missouri (October 2018).

Dr. Washington is the author of the "36.5 Day Challenge" a daily devotional to accomplishing your goals and dreams. Dr. Washington is also the author of "Trophy Wife, Powerless Life."

Washingtonbusinessconsultants@gmail.com
Google Voice: (708) 762-9943
LinkedIn: Dr. Maudia Washington
IG Account: faithjourney9
Twitter Account: @FaithJourney9

Anstrice Mcmillian Epps is a woman of god that is called to prophetic ministry. She has a drive given by god to demonstrate and teach God's people how to live in their God-given authority. She has a passion for helping women, to heal and be restored by God to led them into their destiny. She is the founder and creator of She Writes For God blog. Anstrice is a loving wife and mother of two children. She attends progressive MBC where her pastor is F. Bernard Fuller. Currently, she resides in Raeford, NC.

Phone Number is 910-250-8750
Email address is info@shewritesforGod.com
www.shewritesforGod.com
Follow on: Facebook-@ ShewritesforGod & @AnstriceMEpps
Instagram-@ AnstriceMEpps and @ShewritesforGod
Twitter @ ShewritesforGod

Carolyn Boler is the second of six children to the late Adam Boler and Lucinda Key Boler. She has been called since eight years old. She has gone through many trials and tribulations. But God! She later graduated from Oral Roberts University with a Bachelors in Business Administration, a Masters of Divinity and Pastoral Counseling. She is currently pursuing her Doctorate Degree at Capella University. She is completing her Board Certified Chaplaincy at Carolinas Medical. She is also employed as a Diversity and Inclusion Leader at American Airlines. Carolyn loves to volunteer and feed homeless families at Crisis Ministries. She is a trainer, and Life Coach for Jesus. She also served at the YMCA, and Women's Shelters. Carolyn enjoys evangelizing and empowering God's people. She serves as a former Associate Pastor at Pleasant Ridge Baptist and Liberty World Outreach. She is a purity with Purpose Graduate and Facilitator. Carolyn Boler is an ordained Prophetess underneath Apostles Larry and LaShawn Stokes, in Tulsa, Oklahoma. On the side, she's a Mary Kay and Paparazzi Facilitator. Carolyn donates and builds up young ladies and women.

Carolyn Boler is the founder of Boler Empowerment Center that teaches Biblical, Prophetic Wisdom, and Life Skills. She also founded Carolyn Boler Ministries International and Enjoying Your Season Single's Ministry. She also does workshops on wholeness. Carolyn ministered on a series of "21 Days Of Poverty To Purpose," and "5 Days Of Grace" on periscope and Facebook.

Email: CarolynBoler@gmail.com, website being developed Feb 2019: CarolynBoler.com

Facebook @Carolyn Boler

Twitter @CarolynBoler

Instagram @CarolynBoler

Periscope @CarolynBoler

LinkedIn @Carolyn Boler

Alex Harding III was born and raised in Jeanerette, Louisiana. Alex has always had a passion for reading and writing literature. By the tender age of 8 years old, he began writing story books and music. By middle school he was voted most talented by his class. By high school, he was opening performances for major artists. After graduation, in 2007 he took his music to the next level. By 2010, he had songs on Louisiana radio stations and a huge buzz known for his smash dance single "Dumb Wit It," which is considered a classic with over one million YouTube streams and large notoriety throughout the entire state of Louisiana and surrounding states in the southwest region. Alex currently writes a lot of music and is still recording and scout's fresh talent for mentorship. Alex has three beautiful kids (oldest to youngest) Markei Nykiren, Kamryn Alexis, and Ayden King. Alex is a lifelong and active member at Our Lady of the Rosary Catholic Church in Jeanerette, La. where he is an active lector of the gospel and assists the Youth Religion Catechism Program. Alex plans to continue writing more books to spread the Gospel of Jesus Christ. Alex still resides in Louisiana.

Contact Info: Alexharding337@gmail.com
Facebook: Alex Harding

1 Samuel 30: 8 says, "And David inquired to the Lord shall I pursue, Shall I overtake thee, and the Lord answered Pursue and thou shall overtake thee and without fail recover all."

Alexander Young is a very peculiar person in a unique way. Often misunderstood, ignored, but I can tell you there is more than meets the eye with this Anointed Man of God. Alexander was born and raised on the South side of Chicago, IL. He is a proud father of four boys, a very appreciative man to a strong supportive woman of God/ Fiancé, and a minister of the Gospel.

Mr. Young served twelve years in the United States Army to include three combat tours to Iraq. He was honorably discharged with the rank of Sergeant. He has well deservedly earned numerous medals, badges, and awards during the time of service. After the military, minister Young went to further his education. He obtained an Associates degree in Human Resource Management and a Bachelors in Business Management. Alexander does not take his calling lightly. He humbly accepts his role as a chosen vessel for the kingdom.

Alexander Young received his calling to the ministry in July 2007 but, did not walk in or accept his calling until December 2013. He has dealt with many obstacles and setbacks throughout his time after the military service. That did not stop him from accomplishing his goals. Before Alex became a minister at the church he currently attends, he served in different auxiliaries at a different church. He served as an Usher for the church, in the choir, and in the men's choir. While bouncing back from being homeless, Mr. Young has served within the community. He found himself becoming more successful and achieved many accomplishments. Alexander received a proclamation from the city Mayor, and is a co-author of a book titled "Magnificent Men." He also earned his Ordination of Elevation from Minister to Elder. Not only does he serve in the capacity of a minister at his current church but also, he serves as the Bishop's Adjutant. Alexander Young has a vision for the Kingdom. His purpose which is for everyone to receive the Salvation and see the Glory of the Lord work in their lives. He has a passion for helping the homeless, and he also has a passion for relationship building. Alexander walks in his purpose not to be liked but it is necessary. He will do whatever it takes to edify the Kingdom.

Contact info: email: alexmyoung55@gmail.com
Church: Family of Faith Worship Center, Clarksville, TN Pastor Bishop Anthony Alfred

La Rose Angela Richardson is the wife of Richard Richardson, and mother of Satara Cowan. She has one granddaughter, Allara Cowan; She has lived in the Southeast Georgia area all her life. La Rose has worked in the nursing field for a total of twenty-two years. First as a Certified Nursing Aide for eight years, then going further in her studies for Practical Nursing. She graduated from Southeastern Technical Institute in June 1997 with a degree in Practical Nursing. She worked at a local nursing home in Vidalia, GA for 14 years as a L.P.N. After marrying her husband Richard Richardson on July 10, 2009, she moved to the city of Alma, GA. In June 2018, she moved to the city of Baxley, GA where she now resides with her husband. She went to Crossland Christian University, Alma, GA campus. Later she graduated with a Master of Arts Degree in Theology on May 30, 2015, in Orlando, FL. She was ordained on May 29,2015, at an Ordination service before graduation at Cross land Christian University. She is a poetry writer with several poems published in "Our Great Modern Poets." She continued to pursue her education later graduating with a Doctors Degree in Theology from Cross land Christian University all while serving at her local church and teaching Sunday School to the 6 to 9-year-old children.

She joined the prayer line "Tongues of fire" in November 2018 with Prophetess Kimberly Moses. She has been greatly empowered by praying in tongues for an hour daily. She is one of the authors, "It Cost Me Everything," which is her first co-author writing. She is writing on the subject "Anger" because of something that happened in her life. When she was younger, her Father had caused her great pain and distress, because he walked away and left the whole family when she was only 13 years old. It took the help of the Lord to help her release and forgive her dad, even after his death in 2015. It hasn't been easy, but with God's help, she has been able to overcome her anger and be at peace.

Email: ministerrich0628@gmail.com
Facebook: Angela Richardson

Elder Bridget Denise Jefferson was born in December 16, 1967, in Buffalo, New York. She was baptized at the age of 10 at Mt Aarat Baptist Church in Buffalo, New York. She gave her Life to Christ and surrendered to the will of God and was filled with the Holy Ghost in July of 2015. She was fire baptized in 2016. Bridget is a strong anointed Seer of God and intercessory prayer warrior. She lives in Lithonia, Georgia.

She is the daughter of the late Brenda Joyce Burroughs and the Late Oscar Henry Burroughs. She has two older brothers Nathaniel Joe Stokes and Craig Burroughs. She is also the Granddaughter of the late Rev Henry O Burroughs & late Josephine Burroughs; and the late Edward H Hodge and late Della Mae Hodge.

Bridget is married to Overseer Bryndon Duran Jefferson. He is the Pastor and Founder of Forever Faithful Christian Ministries in Atlanta, Georgia. They have a blended family of eight children and five grandchildren. Bridget attends Ashford University and obtaining a Healthcare Administration BA Program. She works in Administration at Emory Hospital in Atlanta, Georgia.

bridget.jefferson67@gmail.com
honeybee_jefferson Instagram

References

1. "Addiction." Merriam-Webster.com. Accessed January 9, 2019. https://www.merriam-webster.com/dictionary/addiction.

2. "Incorporating Tobacco Cessation with Health Promotion Activities in a Psychosocial Rehabilitation Clubhouse." www.umassmed.edu Accessed January 10, 2019. https://www.umassmed.edu/globalassets/center-for-mental-health-services-research/documents/products-publications/posters/wellness/incorporating_tobacco_cessation.pdf

3. "What Drinking Costs You Over the Course of Your Life." https://www.thebalanceeveryday.com/what-lifetime-of-drinking-costs-4142309 Accessed January 10, 2019. https://www.thebalanceeveryday.com/what-lifetime-of-drinking-costs-4142309

4. "Adultery." Merriam-Webster.com. Accessed January 8, 2019. https://www.marriam-webter.com/dictionary/adultery.

5. "Alcoholism." Merriam-Webster.com. Accessed December 19, 2018. https://www.merriam-webster.com/dictionary/alcoholism

6. 40 Day Fast by Rebecca L. King, Accessed December 19,2018

7. "Anger." Merriam-Webster.com. Accessed December 19, 2018. https://www.merriam-webster.com/dictionary/anger.

8. Behavioral Science & Law Journal for statistics, Accessed on December 18, 2018. https:// www.minipost.com

9. Spiritual Intervention by Kimberly Ray Accessed December 19, 2018

10. "Depression." Merriam-Webster.com. Accessed January 6, 2019. https://www.merriam-webster.com/dictionary/depression

11. Simpson, Amy. "Addressing Depression and Suicide in Your Church." Christian History | Learn the History of Christianity & the Church. July 06, 2018. Accessed January 06, 2019. https://www.christianitytoday.com/pastors/2013/april-online-only/addressing-depression-and-suicide-in-your-church.html

12. "Tactic." Merriam-Webster.com. Accessed January 6, 2019. https://www.merriam-webster.com/dictionary/tactic

13. "Disobedience." Merriam-Webster.com. Accessed January 24, 2019. https://www.merriam-webster.com/dictionary/disobedience.

14. "Divorce." Merriam-Webster.com. Accessed January 29, 2019. https://www.merriam-webster.com/dictionary/divorce.

15. "Domestic Violence." Merriam-Webster.com. Accessed January 5, 2019. https://www.merriam-webster.com/dictionary/domesticviolence .

16. "20 people per minute are physically abused". https://ncadv.org. Accessed January 5, 2019. https://ncadv.org/statistics

17. "Home is the most dangerous place for women." https://www.unodc.org. Accessed January 5, 2019. https://www.unodc.org/unodc/en/frontpage/2018/November/home-the-most-dangerous-place-for-women-with-majority-of-female-homicide-victims-worldwide-killed-by-partners-or-family--unodc-study-says.html?ref=fs1

18. "Envy." Merriam-Webster.com. Accessed January 13, 2019. https://www.merriam-webster.com/dictionary/envy.

19. "Fear." Merriam-Webster.com. Accessed December 23, 2018. https://www.merriam-webster.com/dictionary/fear.

20. Medically Reviewed by Timothy J. Legg, PhD, CRNP—Written by The Healthline Editorial Team https://www.healthline.com/health/stress-and-anxiety (accessed January 5, 2019)

21. BibleHelps.com. https://biblehelpsinc.org/publication/the-paralyzing-power-of-fear/ (accessed December 23, 2018).

22. Fornication." Merriam-Webster.com, Merriam-Webster, www.merriam-webster.com/dictionary/fornication. Accessed 22 Dec. 2018.

23. Cafourek, John. "Breaking Free from Sexual Addictions." United Church of God. February 06, 2005. https://www.ucg.org/united-news/breaking-free-from-sexual-addictions. Accessed December 22, 2018.

24. "Gluttony." Merriam-Webster.com. Accessed January 10, 2019. https://www.merriam-webster.com/dictionary/gluttony.

25. "90% of Americans don't like to cook—and it's costing them thousands each year." www.cnbc.com. Accessed January 10, 2019. https://www.cnbc.com/2017/09/27/how-much-americans-waste-on-dining-out.html

26. "Guilt." Merriam-Webster.com. Accessed January 8, 2019. https://www.merriam-webster.com/dictionary/guilt.

27. "Incest." Merriam-Webster.com. Accessed February 1, 2019. https://www.merriam-webster.com/dictionary/incest.

28. "What's the translation for these Hebrew words: "Elohel Helel" or "Eloel Helel"?". Accessed February 1, 2019. https://www.quora.com/Whats-the-translation-for-these-Hebrew-words-Elohel-Helel-or-Eloel-Helel

29. "Incest." Merriam-Webster.com. Accessed January 14, 2019. https://www.merriam-webster.com/dictionary/incest.

30. "The Problem With Incest. Evolution, morality and the politics of abortion." www.psychologytoday.com. Accessed January 14, 2019. https://www.psychologytoday.com/us/blog/animals-and-us/201210/the-problem-incest

31. "Impact of Europe's Royal Inbreeding: Part II." www.medicalbag.com. Accessed January 14,

2019. https://www.medicalbag.com/grey-matter/part-ii-british-royals-house-of-kissing-cousins/article/472430/.

32. "Incest Laws and Criminal Charges." www.criminaldefenselawyer.com. Accessed January 14, 2019. https://www.criminaldefenselawyer.com/resources/criminal-defense/white-collar-crime/incest-laws-criminal-charges.htm

33. "Long-term effects of incest: life events triggering mental disorders in female patients with sexual abuse in childhood." www.ncbi.nlm.nih.gov. Accessed January 14, 2019. https://www.ncbi.nlm.nih.gov/pubmed/1393719

34. "Lust." Merriam-Webster.com. Accessed January 2, 2019. https://www.merriam-webster.com/dictionary/lust.

35. "Lie." Merriam-Webster.com. Accessed January 3, 2019. https://www.merriam-webster.com/dictionary/lie.

36. 18 U.S. Code § 1621 - Perjury generally. www.law.cornell.edu. Accessed January 4, 2019. https://www.law.cornell.edu/uscode/text/18/1621

37. "What Christians need to know about sexual abuse" www.ucg.org/united, accessed January 1, 2019.

38. "Molestation", Merriam-Webster.com, www.Merriam-Webster.com/dictionary/molest, accessed December 20, 2018.

39. Darkness to Light www.d2l.org/wp-content/uploads/2017/01/all_statistics_20150619.pdf, accessed December 20, 2018.

40. " Shame: A Concealed, Contagious, and Dangerous Emotion" www.psychologytoday,com/us/blog/intense-emotions-and-strong-feelings/201104/shame-concealed-contagious-and-dangerous-emotion, accessed December 31, 2018.

41. "The Second Assault", www.theatlantic.com/health/archive/2015/12/sexual-abuse-victims-obesity/420186, accessed January 1, 2019.

42. "Perversion." Merriam-Webster.com. Accessed January 26, 2019. https://www.merriam-webster.com/dictionary/perversion.

43. "Broke." Merriam-Webster.com. Accessed January 26, 2019. https://www.merriam-webster.com/dictionary/broke.

44. "Evil." Merriam-Webster.com. Accessed January 26, 2019. https://www.merriam-webster.com/dictionary/evil.

45. "Action." Merriam-Webster.com. Accessed January 26, 2019. https://www.merriam-webster.com/dictionary/action.

46. "Sexual." Merriam-Webster.com. Accessed January 26, 2019. https://www.merriam-webster.com/dictionary/sexual.

47. Strong LL.D S.T.D, James. 1996. The New Strong's Complete Dictionary of Bible Words. Nashville, Tennessee: Thomas Nelson Publishers.

48. Conner, Kevin J. The Foundations of Christian Doctrine. Conner Ministries. Accessed January 26, 2019.

49. "Atheist." Merriam-Webster.com. Accessed January 26, 2019. https://www.merriam-webster.com/dictionary/atheist.

50. "Pride." Merriam-Webster.com. Accessed January 26, 2019. https://www.merriam-webster.com/dictionary/pride.

51. "Prostitution." Merriam-Webster.com. Accessed January 14, 2019. https://www.merriam-webster.com/dictionary/prostitution.

52. "What is a soul tie?" http://www.ministeringdeliverance.com Accessed January 14, 2019. http://www.ministeringdeliverance.com/soul_ties.php

53. "Rape." Merriam-Webster.com. Accessed January 14, 2019. https://www.merriam-webster.com/dictionary/rape.

54. " Psychological disorder." Merriam-Webster.com. Accessed January 14, 2019. https://www.merriam-webster.com/dictionary/psychologicaldisorder.

55. "Aloofness." Merriam-Webster.com. Accessed January 14, 2019. https://www.merriam-webster.com/dictionary/aloofness.

56. "Revenge." Merriam-Webster.com. Accessed January 8, 2019. https://www.merriam-webster.com/dictionary/revenge.

57. "Sloth." Merriam-Webster.com. Accessed January 13, 2019. https://www.merriam-webster.com/dictionary/sloth.

58. "Steal." Merriam-Webster.com. Accessed January 15, 2019. https://www.merriam-webster.com/dictionary/steal.

59. "Strife." Merriam-Webster.com. Accessed January 15, 2019. https://www.merriam-webster.com/dictionary/strife.

60. "Soul." Merriam-Webster.com. Accessed January 15, 2019. https://www.merriam-webster.com/dictionary/soul.

61. "Tie." Merriam-Webster.com. Accessed January 15, 2019. https://www.merriam-webster.com/dictionary/tie.

62. "Witchcraft." Merriam-Webster. Accessed December 17, 2018. https://www.merriam-webster.com/dictionary/witchcraft.

63. Strong, James, LL.D.,S.T.D. Strong's Complete Word Study Concordance. Edited by Warren Baker. Chattanooga, TN:

AMG Publishers, 2004. Pharmakeia (5331)-Greek word for witchcraft.

64. Strong, James, LL.D.,S.T.D. Strong's Complete Word Study Concordance. Edited by Warren Baker. Chattanooga, TN: AMG Publishers, 2004. Pharmacy (5332).

Index

A

abnormalities, 190
abortion, 124–25
addictions, 3–5, 8, 21–22, 82
adultery, 9, 16, 18, 268
alcohol, 3–4, 21–22
Aloofness, 190
angels, 52, 76
anger, 27–30, 33, 38, 59, 79, 128, 155, 161, 164, 252
anxiety attacks, 184
appointment, 123
Atheist, 171

B

behavior, 27, 72, 167–68, 198, 201
bitterness, 71, 79, 82–83, 158–59, 196, 252
blessings, 50, 126–27
blood, 86, 103, 160, 235, 241

C

childhood, 38, 154, 157–59
cigarettes, 4

condemnation, 119
conflict, 215–16
confusion, 71, 105, 164, 220–21
control, 21, 32, 62, 86, 130, 181–82, 232, 235–36
couple, 72, 122–23, 198–99, 206, 231, 234–35
court, 78
curses, 106, 233, 235–36

D

damage, 152
dark secret, 154–55
daughters, 52, 243
death, 10, 52, 113, 142, 170, 184, 204, 236
deception, 9–10, 17, 105, 129, 149, 189, 222, 230
deliverance, 22, 41, 146, 150, 168, 245
depression, 40–41, 44–46, 48, 103, 124, 144, 161, 164
destiny, 29, 33, 70, 94
diabetes, 113, 115, 142, 158, 204
disobedience, 50–51, 53–54, 56
divisions, 128, 214
divorce, 5–6, 18, 35, 46, 58, 145, 269
doctrine, 143
doors, 99, 132, 152, 188
dreams, 163, 235, 258
drunkards, 143, 210

E

education, 252–54

emotions, 27, 38, 95, 154, 157–58, 190, 219
envious, 89, 91, 93
errands, 124
escape, 52, 89

F

failures, 95, 119
faith, 13, 94, 116, 207
family, 21, 27–28, 33, 41, 44, 55, 62, 69, 76, 104–5, 136–38, 144, 189–90, 211, 217
family reunion, 61
fear, 70, 94–98, 100, 102, 142, 191, 247
fool, 14, 214, 216
forgive, 26, 29–30, 37–38, 87, 100, 247
fornication, 101, 106
freedom, 38–39, 95, 119, 164

G

glasses, 79
gluttony, 112–14
gospel, 93, 170, 238
guilt, 12, 60, 118–20, 124, 143, 161, 271

H

heartbroken, 138
heaven, 1, 66, 129, 254
Holy Ghost, 252

homeless, 233
hopelessness, 40–41, 43
house, 25, 55, 59, 75, 212, 233
husband, 11, 35, 63, 67, 104, 125, 141, 198, 233, 243

I

idolatry, 126, 128, 229
idols, 110, 132–33, 221, 224
incest, 135–36, 139
intoxication, 189
isolation, 41, 43

J

jealousy, 128, 155, 162, 182, 229
Jesus, 8, 12, 68, 84, 86–87, 116–17, 119, 124–25, 133–34, 146, 159–60, 163–64, 166, 181, 235
joy, 39, 71, 77, 89, 146, 164

K

knowledge, 151

L

laziness, 134, 206
liars, 149–50
lust, 13–14, 18, 20, 101, 105, 140–44, 146–47, 161, 169, 272

M

marriage, 12, 18, 53, 59, 62, 162, 197, 199, 214
masturbation, 134
memories, 154
mentorship, 34, 36
mind, 43, 48–50, 83, 100, 105, 110, 155, 157–58, 164, 181, 190–91, 216, 219, 222–23, 225
ministry, 42, 44, 126, 130, 238, 241, 243, 246, 249, 255
molestation, 154–57, 159, 161, 164, 172
murder, 30, 89, 92

N

nations, 188, 238, 240

O

offense, 30, 189
oily, 15, 42, 44, 106, 144, 205

P

pain, 26, 35–36, 157–58, 164, 172–73
parole, 64, 92
passion, 1, 245–46, 255, 262, 264
pastor, 8, 67
personality, 190
perversion, 161, 166–67, 171, 253
pizza, 205, 207

poverty, 112, 114, 158, 204, 260

power, 12, 56, 70, 103, 117, 124, 129–30, 139, 142, 159, 168, 174, 196, 237

pray, 22–23, 25, 31–32, 48, 100, 124, 146–47, 201, 208, 213

prayer meetings, 249

prayers, 26, 36, 86–87, 93, 139, 145, 150–51, 180, 201, 217, 226, 245, 248

pride, 11, 20, 114, 132, 142, 176–80, 182, 274

prostitution, 183–84

R

rage, 82, 164, 229

rape, 189–90

rape victims, 190

rebellion, 229–30

rejection, 104, 155, 221

remembrance, 177

reprobate mind, 143

responsibility, 167

restoration, 30

retaliation, 29, 31, 196

revenge, 83, 195–97

S

secrets, 120, 161, 226

selfishness, 9

sex, 9, 19, 54, 105, 110, 132, 159, 169, 183, 185

shame, 12, 94, 156–57, 161, 164, 178

sickness, 39, 113, 127, 158
sins, 1–2, 9, 12, 26, 52, 101, 105–6, 119, 138, 156, 169, 173–74, 210, 226, 229
sisters, 7, 45, 76–77, 243, 251
sorcery, 128, 155, 228
sorrows, 40, 104, 128
soul, 87, 157–59, 163–64, 184, 196, 219, 246
soul ties, 19, 103, 184, 219–20, 222–23, 226, 235
strife, 128, 155, 214–16
suicide, 42, 103, 144
support, 99, 162–63, 255

T

tactics, 41–42
teachers, 132, 170
television, 84, 123, 205, 207, 212, 217, 240
temptations, 13, 109, 140
thief, 169, 171
tongues, 181, 186
torment, 103, 144
transgressions, 89

U

unbreakable, 220
unconsciousness, 189

V

victimization, 87
victims, 22, 159, 190
vindictive spirit, 196
violence, 87, 215
voice, 43, 84, 172, 175, 213, 220

W

weight loss, 53
wickedness, 83, 128, 210
wife, 9–11, 17–18, 20, 52, 58, 104, 106, 128
witchcraft, 228–30, 235–36, 276
words curses, 236
work performance, 204
world, 2, 20, 30, 41–42, 92, 169–70, 172, 230, 236, 238

Y

yoke, 147

www.ingramcontent.com/pod-product-compliance
Lightning Source LLC
Chambersburg PA
CBHW071302110526
44591CB00010B/752